CHARACTER-BUILDING · OMA'S · STORIES

By Oma Ellis
with Rita Dawson

Oma's Character-Building Stories

by Oma Ellis with Rita Dawson

©1992 Word Aflame Press
Hazelwood, MO 63042

Cover Design by Tim Agnew

Printed in United States of America.

Printed by

Library of Congress Cataloging-in-Publication Data

Ellis, Oma.
    Oma's character building stories / by Oma Ellis with Rita Dawson.
       p.   cm.
    ISBN 0-932581-89-7 :
    1. Ellis, Oma. 2. Pentecostal churches—United States—Clergy—
Biography. I. Dawson, Rita. II. Title.
BX 8762.Z8E45 1992
289.9'4'092—dc20
[B]   91-36230
                                          CIP

Contents

Preface

You hold in your hands a sacrifice, a legacy of love and concern from a dear and precious saint of God. A few months after completing this book Sister Ellis laid down her worn-out tools and quietly slipped away. Only then did her labors cease.

This book, her fourth, was by far the most difficult. It was written while totally bedfast. She could no longer sit up enough to use her typewriter, so it was written laboriously in a prone position in longhand. When my husband drove me to Mitchell, South Dakota, to pick up the manuscript I noted a severe redness of her eyes. When I questioned her about it she said her eyelashes were curling inward and irritating her eyeballs. I silently groaned with compassion. I wonder if anyone will ever really realize or fully appreciate what these chapters cost this dear sister.

She confided in me that this was her last effort to win her loved ones to the Lord. "They didn't want me to talk to them about their souls, but I believe they will read my book. I am inserting messages for specific reasons."

I prayed for weeks, even months before I ever rewrote the first chapter. I have written so much about this family that I almost feel as if I am a part of it. Though I took great liberties in arranging and rearranging her stories, I was very careful to leave her little Bible studies basically as she recorded them.

Please give heed to her admonitions. I repeatedly got the impression that many tears and many prayers went into this volume. This is a treasure more valuable than if she had left houses, lands, and wealth. This is an inheritance—not only for her family but for all who read and believe.

> Rita Dawson
> March 2, 1991
> Weedpatch, California

Editor's Note: Two weeks after completing her work on this book Rita Dawson passed away.

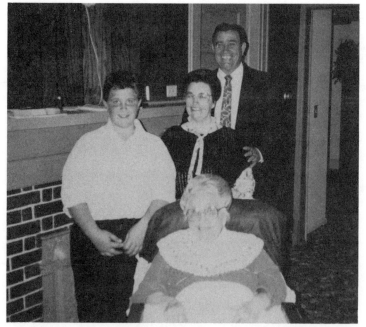

Rev. Dearl Dawson, Sis. Rita Dawson, David Dawson (son) and Oma Ellis, October 1989. The Dawsons came to pick up the manuscript at Mitchell, South Dakota.

Introduction

Character is not born in a new baby. But all the potential is there. A baby's behavior, personality, and moral constitution are shaped and molded by its environmental influences, experiences, and impressions. The strengths and weaknesses of its ancestors are often developed in the descendant.

I have cause to thank God for the wonderful heritage He gave me. The stories that thrilled, chilled and inspired me in my childhood, plus the experiences of my life that altered my existence, make up the format of this book. I leave them as a legacy to my own descendants, as well as to all who hope for growth in themselves and their loved ones.

I determined to record these stories because of a series of incidents that occurred in a short span of time some years ago.

My great-granddaughter, Denise Uecker, had just finished reading a set of books, *The Little House Series,* by Laura Ingalls Wilder. She came to my little room situated in their home where I have been bedfast for many months. She insisted that I write a book telling about my ancestors the way Laura Ingalls Wilder had written about her childhood. Denise's mother, my granddaughter, Fern Uecker, who has so lovingly provided for my care and comfort, added her opinion. "Grandma, I have been thinking the same thing for a long time. I think you should write all the stories you have told over these many years. Then even our children's children would have them to hand down to their descendants, if Jesus tarries."

"Oh, children," I said, "I could never write a book just for fun or entertainment! Ever since I gave my heart to God, I have tried to do everything for the glory of God."

A few days later my eldest son, Elton, called on the telephone. He had no way of knowing what had been said about a book of my stories being written. But during our conversation he voiced almost the same words. In fact, he insisted that I write such a book.

A few months later my fifth-generation descendant, Michael Shane O'Neal, was born. On Easter Sunday 1986, Reverend James O'Neal and I, his great-great-grand-mother, dedicated him to the Lord. The next day I was talking on the telephone with our secretary of foreign missions, Edwin E. Judd. He asked about my great-grand-daughter, Kelly (Ikerd) O'Neal. I told him we had just dedicated her baby son to the Lord the day before. He remarked, "My! What a great inheritance that young man has by birth."

I am sure Brother Judd was thinking, as I was, about the godly ancestors all the way back to 1896. Little Michael Shane was the seventh generation from my grandfather, Andrew Jackson Harris. When Grandfather received the Holy Ghost, people did not teach that speaking in tongues was the evidence of the infilling of the Holy Ghost, as we understand today. Rather, they simply called it the "gift of tongues," I have been told. Nevertheless, from the time Grandfather Harris received his Holy Ghost experience he was a changed man, influencing all around him and generations to come!

The question was asked during the writing of *Strength through Struggle,* the autobiography of Fred Kinzie, "When does God start working in a life? At the baptismal waters? At the infilling of the Holy Ghost?" The Kinzies found that with them, God started in their young childhood.

In my research I have found my Holiness roots go back to my Grandfather Harris. Three years after he received the Spirit, he lay upon his deathbed. He laid hands upon my mother six weeks before my birth and dedicated her unborn child to be a Holiness preacher.

I was twenty-four years old when God called me to preach. He gave me a verse of Scripture when I was in a spirit of prayer: "Before I formed thee in the belly I knew thee; and before thou camest forth out of the womb I sanctified thee, and I ordained thee a prophet unto the nations" (Jeremiah 1:5).

At that time, I was so unlearned in the Scriptures that I had no idea where to find those words. I searched and searched but was unable to locate that verse of Scripture. I almost gave up, thinking, That must not be in the Bible. I was very tired and worn when I finally found it in the Book of Jeremiah. I got up from my knees and went to my bedroom. As soon as I fell asleep God gave me my first vision.

Two doors, from the north and south, opened into my bedroom. I could enter from the north porch, walk straight across my room, and exit out onto the south porch. The foot of my bed stood on this walkway from door to door. In my vision I saw Jesus enter the north door. He came and stood with another man at the foot of my bed. Jesus introduced the man as the apostle Paul. The apostle Paul held up what appeared to be letters and told me, "Preach and teach these." Then he walked over to the south door and pressed a box to the wall, depositing his letters in it just as he went out the south door.

After him came another writer, and another. Jesus introduced each of them, and they admonished me to preach and teach their letters. After each man deposited his letter in the box and left, another man would enter. On and on they went until at last I sensed that was all, so I jumped from my bed and reached for those letters.

My vision ended, and I came to myself standing by the south door reaching for the box that held the letters. The vision had been so real that I stood there confused. A few minutes later I noticed my Bible lying on the bed where I had left it. I remembered the box was the size, shape, and color of my Bible! Then it dawned upon me that all those letters were in my Bible. I picked it up and pressed it to my heart.

From that time on I had a great hunger to read the Word of God. The characters in the Bible seemed to be my personal friends. I cherished those letters and determined to preach and teach them.

Long before this vision altered my life, God had been preparing me for my life's vocation. My parents were strict disciplinarians, and my Grandmother Harris awed me with her stories of my ancestors. My character was being molded and shaped even when I was unaware of how desperately I would need the very qualities they were instilling in me.

I have divided these stories into three categories: first, my ancestry and inheritance (spiritual as well as literal); then my childhood memories; and finally my adult experiences I felt would influence posterity. Grandma Harris supplied most of my ancestral information. Not only did her stories thrill me as a child, but my son Elton said he could remember listening to her snake story when he was a seven-year-old child.

People told me that my Grandfather Harris's last earthly act was his dedication prayer for me. My Grandfather Francis died long before my birth, and my Grandmother Francis died when I was four years old. I was twenty-nine years old when Grandma Harris died in 1928. Grandfather Harris left me a rich inheritance of faith, but it was Grandma Harris's faithful repetition of events that has enriched my life and the lives of their other descendants.

Those who read this book must remember that this is not presented as a literary masterpiece. Rather it is a collection of stories that had a part in molding my character, and by repetition, will help to shape the character of all who read these pages.

Oma Ellis

Mitchell, South Dakota

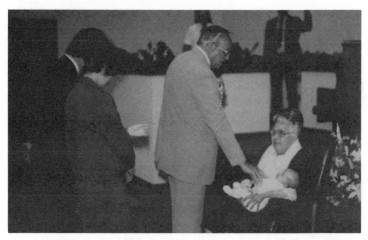

Easter Sunday, 1986 dedicating great-great grandson Michael Shane O'Neal; Rev. James O'Neal and Oma Ellis.

Sis. Rita Dawson, October 1989 visiting Oma Ellis in Mitchell, South Dakota working on the manuscript.

PART ONE

$\mathscr{A}$NCESTORS

Thomas Jefferson Francis was my father's dad, and Andrew Jackson Harris was my mother's dad. Their parents were from Europe, but both of these men were born in the United States. As I researched my genealogy I failed to find any ties to royalty!

In 1984 Ronald Reagan, at that time the president of the United States, visited his ancestral home of Ballyporeen, in the Irish county of Tipperarry. A British genealogist traced his background to a link with the eleventh-century Irish king, Brian Baru, who died saving Ireland from the Vikings. The *Reader's Digest* said in July 1986, "President Reagan was thus tied into European royal lines, making him cousin to Princess Diana and France's President Francois Mitterrand."

I like what the *Digest* writer then said about genealogy: "In the end if genealogy is anything, it is not so much the Webster's defined study of family descent as it is developing a deep appreciation for those who have gone before us. Whether they are princes, or paupers, prisoners or prima donnas, their life stories are treasures to those who patiently and persistently delve into their family history."

Certainly the life stories of my ancestors are treasures to me. Since both of my grandfathers came to Texas in the year 1848, I did a little research on the historical background of that area.

Historical Background

When Texas became a state in 1845, Mexico instantly went to war with her. When the Mexican war ended in 1848 there was a surge of population growth. At this time my grandfathers arrived in Texas, Grandfather Francis from Missouri and Grandfather Harris from Illinois. Both of them were in the U.S. Army.

Within a year of the war's end the U.S. Army had to build a line of forts across the central portion of Texas to protect settlers from attacks by the Apache and Comanche Indians. One of the most important forts in this line was Fort Worth. The expansion of settlements called for another line of forts two hundred miles west of the original line in 1851.

My grandparents all lived in these forts. The best I could do in pinpointing one fort was Fort Davis, the next-to-the-last fort built in West Texas, between Fort Stockton and Fort Bliss. They were associated with other forts also.

Grandfather Francis

I have been told that my Grandfather Francis could not do manual labor because of crippling injuries he received during the war. His trade in life had been cabinet building and designing. My cousin Francis Woodruff (granddaughter of Grandpa Harris's daughter Minty) remembered Grandma Harris saying that Grandpa Francis was a building designer who worked on the forts as an architect. My two younger brothers, Jesse Francis and Tom Francis, told me recently that they were told by our mother, the baby daughter of Andrew Jackson Harris, that both of our grandfathers were Texas Rangers. When Grandpa Francis and his family lived in a fort, he was assigned as the officer over the fort. He would stay with the women and children defending the fort while Grandpa Harris would serve as the officer over the scout force on Indian raids.

By the census of 1860, Texas had one of the largest populations in the nation.

Texans used less slaves than other Southern states. Slaves were found mostly in East Texas and the coastal regions. Plantation farming was profitable only in East Texas. Slaves in other areas served only as household servants. Because of their Christian belief the Francis and Harris families did not have slaves.

Each family did have a black nanny who helped care for the large family of children. These nannies loved the children and the children loved them. I remember being glad my grandparents did not believe in slaves. I heard terrible stories of how cruel masters made the poor people suffer, and my tender heart just could not bear the thought of being a partaker in such things. I was a very sensitive child, and I am sure the slave stories were instrumental in helping to shape my character.

Life in Texas during the Civil and Indian wars was both exciting and hazardous. It was said that "forted up" families could live without bread. There was an abundance of pecans and walnuts, and the women ground these nuts to make their bread. When there was a shortage of beef, the hunters filled the larders with fish, wild turkeys, prairie chickens, quail, antelope, and bison from the surrounding country.

During World War II we experienced a shortage of wheat and learned to make bread using nuts, as they did in my grandparents' day.

Grandma Francis

When I was four years old my grandmother on my father's side of the family died. I know very little about her personally, but my research about the women of that era sheds light on my grandmother's life and times.

Those women of the forts proved their resourcefulness in every crisis. They were too far from towns to make periodic purchases of food, clothing, and medicines. To their credit they proved that "necessity is the mother of invention." They changed deerskin into soft, pliable buckskin, from which they made trousers, moccasins, and gloves. One historian said they even made gray, black, or brown hairnets using hair from horse's tails! When wool or cotton was available they spun thread, wove cloth, and cut and sewed garments. They made their own candles and soap from lye, which they leached from wood ashes.

In my lifetime I helped my mother make soap from ashes. We also made hominy from dried corn, using ashes. I am sure Grandma Francis was proficient in this art, for it was Grandma Harris who taught us how to do it.

When sickness struck the forts these pioneer women

concocted medicinal brews from herbs. When doctors were not available for childbirth, they served as midwives. If a sickness was a life-or-death situation requiring a doctor, a settler would sometimes have to travel hundreds of miles. Labor, hardships, and the ever-present danger of Indian attacks were the frontier woman's daily lot.

The women who lived in forts were taught how to survive if they were ever captured. If they were able to escape they were told to travel east, toward the rising of the sun, because the Indians lived west of the forts. There came a day when this information was needed, for some of the Francis women were captured. Most of the captives were scalped, but two women escaped. They were traveling east when the scouts from the fort found them.

Grandpa Harris

Recently, I read a book that brought back a lot of memories of things my Grandma Harris had told me when I was a child. In this history book was a report by Texas Ranger C. L. Nevill, commander of Company E. He had in his charge some members of the outlaw band connected to Billy the Kid. Nevill said one of his officers, Corporal Harris, caught these men desperately trying to dig out of the fort using a spoon! They had dug to the depth of a man's arm when apprehended. My heart leaped when I read about Corporal Harris, for my grandma had told this very tale!

Grandpa Harris was loyal and served his country well. He established a good name for his descendants. As a Texas Ranger he served with courage and bravery. At his side was an equally brave and courageous wife named Elizabeth. Francis Woodruff told me the story of how they met.

21

The wagon master for whom the young A. J. Harris worked had given him a special assignment: drive the wagon occupied by two widows that joined their wagon train. The older woman was a Mrs. Ramsey who had lost her husband while crossing the Atlantic with her family from Scotland. Scurvy, a common killer in those days, was said to be the cause of his death. Eventually Mrs. Ramsey and her two sons and one daughter settled in Arkansas. The daughter met and married a man named Danell. Their marriage was short-lived, for after only two weeks, Mr. Danell died from a plague. Mrs. Ramsey left her sons in Arkansas and was escorting her daughter to visit her late husband's relatives. And wagon trains were practically the only means of transportation.

Harris did not fail to notice that the younger widow was graceful, resourceful, dutiful, and beautiful! The hardships of the trail failed to prevent him from falling in love with this lovely lady with the porcelain white skin, pink cheeks, violet blue eyes, and glistening black hair. After the trip ended he continued to visit young Elizabeth, courting her fervently until she consented to be his bride. This union produced three sons and seven daughters. The boys were named Bob, Gee, and Jack. The girls were Jane McPherson, Rena Russell, Rachel Adams, Fanny Phelps, Viney Crabtree, Minty Spurgeon, and Nicey Francis, my mother.

Minty Spurgeon's daughter, Winnie, married Roy Jones. Before her marriage, Winnie lived nearly all her life with A. J. and Elizabeth Harris. After marrying Jones, Winnie continued her close association with them. They moved to Sherman, Texas, to be near her parents, and they assisted in Grandma Harris's care after Grandpa died. Their daughter, Francis Woodruff, told me much about our grandfather.

Grandpa Harris, though not wealthy, was generous enough to donate land for a township where Lipan was built in Hood County, Texas. I was interested to learn of my grandfather's generosity, because I have found that people with a generous nature are usually more open to the Spirit of God.

Besides his exploits with Billy the Kid, my grandfather also had close proximity to another famous American, Mr. Charles Goodnight, known as the father of the Texas Panhandle. From the years 1860 to 1896, according to Grandma Harris, these two men were together in various adventures.

By 1896, my grandfather Harris's health had broken. Since he was a Civil War veteran, the U.S. government advised him to do some traveling by wagon with a man named Silas Stone. While on this trip they met a group of Holiness people. Grandfather was thoroughly converted and healed of his ailments. He returned home preaching holiness and praying for the sick. He had only three years to teach his family the power of prayer. But those teachings have reached into the 1990s!

Twenty-seven years after his death my mother and grandmother told me about Grandpa Harris's deathbed prayer: "Lord, I ask Thee to call this child to preach your holy Word. I desire to have a Holiness preacher in my family." When a female was born, the family dismissed the idea of his prayer being fulfilled. In 1926, when I was assisting Brother Matlock in Dallas, Texas, they finally related these facts to me. I can still remember the joy in Grandmother's eyes when she said, "Oma, I wish Grandpa could have lived to know that you are a Holiness preacher!" Aunt Minty chimed in, "It would have made him so happy, for when he left us he was the only one who was Holiness in our family." This reminder really encouraged my heart in the midst of my persecutions and renewed my gratefulness for the spiritual inheritance left me by my Grandpa Harris!

Grandma Harris

Not long after Grandfather died, Grandma Harris and Aunt Minty Spurgeon were converted to Holiness. Aunt Minty told me an interesting story about herself and Grandma. It seems a man stopped by their home while traveling for his health. The two women witnessed to him about holiness, insisting that he repent of his sins and yield his heart to God. Then they prayed for his healing. Aunt Minty was so sure the Lord healed him that she marched into her kitchen and prepared him a steak dinner.

"No, no!" said the man. "My doctor has forbidden me to eat solid food."

"But now God has healed you," said Aunt Minty. "It will not hurt you; it will only give you strength for your journey home."

Sure enough, the food did not harm him. Grandma Harris and Aunt Minty insisted that he stay a few days to prove the Lord had done a work in his body. He left praising God.

In 1918, the U.S. suffered from a great influenza epidemic. It swept from coast to coast in a matter of days, leaving thousands dead. Grandma Harris lived on the old home place in Luella, Texas. Her daughter Minty and son-in-law Will Spurgeon lived in her home and cared for her and the farm. Lizzi, the Spurgeons' daughter, came to visit along with her husband and five children.

While they were there everybody in the household, except Grandma, took the flu. Grandma was more than ninety years old, but she cooked and cared for all of them. The doctor came one morning and discovered that Grandmother was sick with the flu also. One of the others had recovered enough to take over, so the doctor ordered Grandma to bed, saying, "Don't you dare get out of bed, Mrs. Harris!"

He informed the family that her chances were slim for recovery because of her advanced age and her fatigue from caring for all of them. Young people were dying like flies, and he was very concerned about Grandma. Though he was weary with caring for the sick day and night, he hitched up his one-horse buggy the next day to go check on Grandma. As he drove into the yard he noticed someone was feeling well enough to be rocking in the rocking chair on the front porch. To his consternation he recognized the person to be Grandma Harris.

He leaped from his buggy and rushed to her saying, "Mrs. Harris! I told you not to get out of the bed! Why are you disobeying my orders? Get back in that bed!"

Laughing, Grandma said, "Doctor, I'm not about to get back in that bed. God has healed me and I am a well woman." His examination proved her words to be true. He went away amazed at this remarkable woman.

The last time I talked with her we were standing beside Grandpa Harris's grave. She said, "I am looking for the rapture of God's saints. But if Jesus does tarry, I'll be lying here beside Andy, and we shall be caught up together to meet the Lord."

Grandma Harris was with us until 1928. She claimed to be 102 years old. All her records were lost at sea when her father died while her family was crossing from Scotland to America. There was some controversy about her age, but most of her children agreed she was at least 100 years old, perhaps more.

Her conversion and subsequent faithfulness to the Lord helped to further Grandpa Harris's injunction: "As for me and my house, we will serve the LORD" (Joshua 24:15).

Oma's grandparents (mother's parents) Andrew Jackson Harris and Elizabeth Harris.

$\mathcal{G}$RANDMA $\mathcal{H}$ARRIS'S $\mathcal{S}$TORIES

Telling stories came easy to Grandma Harris. She seemed to be a born storyteller. Her excellent memory coupled with her love for her listeners captivated the attention of adults as well as children. We never felt that she exaggerated. The fire in her eyes and the earnest tone of her voice let us know we were listening to an eyewitness account.

I remember well hearing these tales in my early childhood. Sometimes I shivered with fear, sometimes I cried. Always I treasured the lessons gleaned from these sessions, sitting at my grandmother's feet and listening raptly to each episode, never satisfied, always begging for more. Out of her treasury of countless tales, I have selected three of the most memorable stories she repeated over and over throughout the years.

Grandma's Snake Story
"I always dreaded the times when your grandfather had to leave the fort on an Indian raid. Though each family

27

had a log cabin and all of them were surrounded by the sturdy walls of the fort, there still was an element of fear in our hearts when the men were not there. My loneliness was eased by having the children to care for and talk to.

"On one occasion, when one of the babies was only a few weeks old, I prepared the infant for bed by clothing it in a long-tailed gown, which was the habit in those days. When we picked the baby up we could wrap the long tail of the gown around the child, so that it served as an attached blanket. I placed the baby in my bed so I wouldn't have to get out of the bed when it needed to nurse. My bed was built as a scaffold in the corner of the cabin. Cleats were nailed to the wall for supports and legs were attached to create a sturdy bed and a place for storage under the bed.

"One night I was awakened by the unmistakable feeling of a huge snake slithering into the bed between the baby and me. I froze in fright and horror! I had no one to call upon but God. As I silently, desperately prayed, I felt the reptile coiling itself and settling down between my infant and me. I knew the area was overrun with diamondback rattlesnakes, so I had no doubt about the deadliness of this uninvited guest.

"Any quick movement would invite the serpent to strike the child or me. In an agony of suspense I lay perfectly still, waiting, praying that the thing would go to sleep. When that cold mass had been still for some time I determined it was asleep. Moving very slowly and as softly as possible I gradually eased myself out of the bed without disturbing the coiled snake. Very carefully I lifted the quilt at the foot of the bed and groped for the long tail of my baby's gown. Mentally, I was thanking God that was the style for baby gowns! With a mighty jerk, I yanked my baby from that bed before that reptile could strike. With great haste I deposited the baby in a safe place and grabbed a hoe we used for garden work and snake killing. With a courage I did not realize I possessed I managed to kill that deadly diamondback rattlesnake. Had it not been for that long-tailed gown I don't think I could have saved my baby from that rattler!"

This story never failed to leave Grandma's audience spellbound and bug eyed. We never tired of hearing it, because Grandma told it in such a manner we felt as though we were sitting in that log cabin with her!

Billy the Kid

I liked nothing better than to gather with my parents and Uncle Bob around our well-stoked heater in the living room and listen to Grandma tell about Billy the Kid. She could hold anyone's attention with her narrative of the famous outlaw. To exclude Billy from Grandma's repertoire of tales would be a grave injustice. For the sake of accuracy in names and dates I sent my granddaughter, Fern Uecker, to the library of the city of Mitchell, South Dakota, to get me some historical material regarding Billy the Kid. Reading it was like visiting Grandma!

Billy the Kid died eight years before I was born. Grandma said they called him "the Kid" because he was so young to be such a desperate outlaw.

Everybody knew Billy was an orphan. He was born in 1860 and his father died shortly after his birth. His little Irish mother raised him and a brother who was two years older, for fourteen years. Within a year after his mother's death this fifteen-year-old boy was in trouble with the law.

Nothing in his background to that point indicated he would live a life of crime. He worked at a hotel after he was orphaned, and the owner testified that Billy was the only employee he had ever had who did not steal from him. His schoolteacher was quoted, "He was no more of a problem than any other boy. He was quiet and always willing to help with chores around the schoolroom."

His first brush with the law was a trivial thing. An acquaintance was pulling a trick on a Chinese laundry man. He asked Billy to hide the bundle of clothes. The sheriff decided to teach the boy a lesson by putting him in the jail. Two days later the terrified fifteen-year-old escaped by crawling out the chimney. He was a fugitive from the law from that time forward.

Grandma's account of Billy's sufferings after his escape always made me cry. My mother would admonish me to stop crying, for she felt it was harmful to me. My tender heart went out to that orphan boy who clung to friendships and was so loyal to anyone who was kind to him.

He became a teenage saddle tramp, working when he could as a ranch hand or sheepherder in southeastern Arizona. In 1877, at the age of seventeen, he killed his first man.

Billy was employed at the Camp Grant army post as a civilian teamster. A blacksmith there delighted in teasing the orphan boy. It was commonly reported that he called Billy a pimp. The boy retaliated by calling the blacksmith a name that cast a shadow on his mother's morals. In a rage, the blacksmith threw Billy to the ground. The Kid was wearing a gun and he used it. A witness later said, "He had no choice. He was a boy fighting a man. He had to use his equalizer.''

Not everybody believed Billy acted in self-defense. When the blacksmith died the next day, Billy was placed in the guardhouse. After only a few days Billy escaped.

When he stopped at a spring for a drink of water an Apache Indian stole his horse. He was forced to walk many miles before he came to a ranch house in New Mexico. The story circulated that he arrived in a pathetic shape. He was without boots and his feet were swollen and bleeding. He was half starved and perishing of thirst.

The rancher's wife was touched by the poor boy's condition. She fed and cared for him with a motherly concern. Billy was so moved by this treatment he remained long enough to become deeply attached to this family and they to him. They loaned him a horse when he insisted he must be on his way.

At this point nearly everyone favored the Kid. He was so polite, good humored, and obliging that it was hard to imagine him as a brutal criminal. The general consensus of opinion was that he had started off on the wrong foot. People felt he could have been a prince of a man given the right circumstances. Though my grandparents disagreed with his outlaw traits, they shared the public's sympathy for the young fugitive.

Billy found a friend in John Tunstall, a cattleman, banker, and merchant who hired him to work as a cattle guard. Mr. Tunstall was a partner with a lawyer named McSween and a cattleman named Henry Chisum. The three of them felt they could deal directly with the government as beef suppliers. In Lincoln, a group calling themselves "The House" wanted to dominate the government contracts for beef supplied to army posts and Indian reservations. Having powerful connections in Santa Fe, they used political connivance to obtain a court order to collect a great number of cattle on an outstanding debt.

Tunstall refused to surrender the animals, so the sheriff of Lincoln County sent a posse headed by William Morton to make good the court order. When Tunstall objected to the posse's presence, Morton shot him in the head, killing him instantly. Billy was nearby and witnessed the murder of his friend and benefactor. His fury knew no bounds. Some felt this was the turning point in this downy-faced, smiling cowhand's career.

Billy joined a posse formed by Tunstall's employees to capture the killer. They apprehended Morton and another deputy, promising to return them alive to Lincoln. On the journey Billy and another hired hand killed both of the prisoners and a posse member who tried to protect the prisoners.

At this point public opinion turned against the young orphan outlaw. The brutality shocked many. I could see that his intense loyalty to his friends was the underlying cause. How this loyalty affected me! Even years later I sorrowed for the man who needed to know Jesus.

Sheriff Brady sought to arrest Billy three weeks later as he and others holed up in Tunstall's store. It is said that Billy killed Sheriff Brady during a gun battle. A little later McSween was also killed, ending the Lincoln County war, but Billy had only begun to fight.

Billy assembled a ragtag gang of Civil War relics. Their rampage of stealing stock and general law breaking is history. The name Billy the Kid became a household word.

During this time my Grandpa Harris caught a group

of Billy's men trying to escape from the Fort Davis guard-house. They also tried to get a message out to Billy and the rest of the gang to come and rescue them, but were not successful in that endeavor either. Billy had enough murder warrants following him to be taken to the gallows the minute he was caught, but he managed to escape capture for some time longer.

In the fall of 1880, Billy found another friend in the person of Pat Garrett, a bartender at Fort Sumter. This was to be a fatal friendship. Garrett became the new sheriff of Lincoln County. His duties included apprehending his friend, Billy the Kid.

Garrett soon located Billy and his band of cohorts in an abandoned stone building. He surrounded the building and waited. While the sheriff's men prepared a broiled meal outside, Billy and his men, hungry, weary and desperate, suffered the tantalizing smells as long as they could. Billy surrendered to Garrett, explaining they had no way to prepare food.

It took only one day for the jury in Mesilla to find Billy guilty and sentence him to hang. However, before they could build the gallows, Billy made a stunning escape.

The story of that escape was told and retold. It seems that Pat Garrett was not there, being away from the jail on business. He left in charge a guard named Robert Olinger. When Olinger escorted some prisoners across the street for supper, Billy asked the other guard, J. W. Bell, to take him to the privy. Bell placed handcuffs on his prisoner, not knowing that Billy had an old trick of slipping out of them. He had large wrists and small hands and could get out of a pair of handcuffs in no time at all. This he did, striking Bell with the handcuffs and shooting him with a gun supplied by a sympathizer, so the story was circulated.

Billy went into the sheriff's office, acquired a shotgun, and waited for the other guard. When Olinger arrived Billy called his name and shot him dead when he looked up to the balcony of the jail.

It is said that Billy spent over an hour at the jail dancing, laughing, and joking like nothing ever happened. Nobody dared oppose him. Pat Garrett was not surprised by the report, for he knew him well. He was quoted as saying, "Me and those who knew him best will tell you that in his most savage and dangerous moods his face always wore a smile. He ate and laughed, drank and laughed, rode and laughed, talked and laughed, fought and laughed."

For two and a half months Billy and his gang went free. A rumor reached Pat Garrett that they were seen in a certain area. Garrett knew Billy the Kid had a friend in that place, and fully understanding his loyalty for his friends, Garrett set out with two deputies to the home of Pete Maxwell.

Arriving about midnight, Garrett stationed the deputies outside, and he went inside to Maxwell's bedroom. Sitting on the edge of the bed, he asked Maxwell if he knew the whereabouts of Billy the Kid. Maxwell informed him that the outlaw had gone to a dance with his cowhands.

At about that time the boys returned from the dance. Billy complained of being hungry and they directed him to the boss's kitchen, which was always well stocked. Running barefoot across the yard, Billy noticed the strangers out front. He altered his course and stepped into Maxwell's bedroom.

In the dark, Billy could not see Garrett sitting on the edge of the bed. Garrett later testified that Billy came within two inches of his knee as he asked, "Pete, who is out there?"

Maxwell whispered to Garrett, "That's him!"

Billy immediately became suspicious, and sensing the presence of a third party, quickly drew his revolver. At that moment Garrett claimed the pistol was within a foot of his breast.

The outlaw retreated and cried, "Who's that?" Garrett aimed toward the voice and fired quickly. Billy the Kid fell dead.

Garrett's account of the incident was widely circulated and documented. Killing his own friend had a profound effect upon him. He claimed Billy was the most complex, lonely person he had ever known. His baffling personality defied anyone's description. Pat Garrett went on to become a captain in the Texas Rangers and served with fame throughout the Southwest.

Billy the Kid was dead at the age of twenty-one. His four-year career as a fugitive outlaw blazed a place in history and a place in the heart of a seven-year-old girl. Later, when I came to know the Lord, I learned that the saddest tragedy that can happen to a man in this life is never to know the sympathizing Jesus. His doom is to be lost. Lost forever!

Cynthia Ann Parker

Not everybody is as familiar with the name Cynthia Ann Parker as with Billy the Kid. But Grandma Harris never failed to thrill us with the story of the little girl who was captured by the Comanche Indians. It seems she was related in some way to the Harris side of my family. We haven't any way of proving it, I suppose, but rumor claimed a connection.

The year was 1836. Cynthia Ann was nine years old when she fell into the hands of Indians. They changed her name to Naduah, and when she was a teenager she was married to an Indian chief, Peta Nacona. Three children were born to them. One of them became the Comanche Indian chief Quanah Parker. (He took his mother's name.) A town in the Panhandle, Quanah, Texas, is named after him.

According to Grandma, Cynthia was "rescued" several times. The first time, Grandpa Harris and her uncle were reportedly with the rescue party. But Cynthia did not appreciate being returned to white civilization. Her heartbreaking grief for her Indian babies touched all who observed her. Eventually, Cynthia Ann stole a horse from her uncle. Rumor had it that the horse was the fastest-running horse in the country. With it she outrode all who tried to recapture her.

After this episode, her uncle and all who witnessed her inconsolable sorrow agreed that it was best to let her remain with the Indians, where she seemed to be happy.

She remained with her chosen tribe until the winter of 1860. A group of Texas Rangers, my Grandfather Harris included, and a famous Texas cattleman, Charles Goodnight, attacked the Newkoynees Camp along the Pease River. They took several captives. Among them they found Naduah (Cynthia Ann Parker) and her baby, Prairie Flower. She was once again returned to her uncle but could not adjust to white civilization. Nor could her baby. Prairie Flower died shortly in white captivity.

Cynthia pined for her baby and her Indian family for six months, when, at the age of thirty-seven she died.

How this tale inflamed my childish heart! Though I certainly did not wish to do such a thing myself, my tender feelings were in complete sympathy with the little girl who renounced her white relatives to spend her life with the Indians!

Chapter Three

$\mathcal{M}$Y $\mathcal{I}$NDIAN $\mathcal{B}$LOOD

Since I became bedfast my oldest son, Forrest Elton Ellis, has called me almost every Sunday. Knowing I was working on this book of character-building stories, he asked, "Mama, did you say anything about your Indian blood?"

"No, I did not," I replied. "I remember so little about it. I remember being teased by my boyfriends about being an Indian. The subject never failed to make me angry, a trait I always blamed on my father."

Elton replied, "I think you should include everything you can remember about it anyway. My children and I will appreciate it, and others in the family will feel the same."

Later, while I was talking to Francis Woodruff, she asked, "Oma, what about this Cherokee Indian relationship I've heard about all my life?"

I told her I had heard about it, too, but had no idea where the connection originated, except I knew it wasn't on the Harris side of my family. I did remember hearing that it was from the Francis side of the family. On the other hand, Grandma Harris told me many times that Cynthia Ann Parker's descendants were the most beautiful and handsome people she had ever seen. When anyone mentioned some of relatives as being handsome or beautiful she would say, "That is their Indian blood."

So I really cannot pinpoint the source of my Indian blood. I only know that my dark olive complexion and high cheekbones have brought a lot of teasing my way.

When my parents moved our family from Oklahoma to Live Oak County near Oakville, Texas, we became neighbors to the William Gabrial Ellis family. They had three sons. It was there the teasing really began about my Indian appearance. Jesse Ellis, the oldest son, came to work as a hired hand on my father's farm. He was quite a teaser. One day, I heard him ask my dad if he had inherited any Indian land in Oklahoma. "You and Oma sure look like Indians," he said.

"No," said Father. "You have to be one-quarter Indian to get any of that land. After a research, I found I was only one-sixteenth Indian."

"There now!" I cried to Jesse Ellis, "That makes me only one thirty-second Indian. That isn't considered enough to be called an Indian. I told you I was not an Indian!"

Such a comment would fail to raise my blood pressure now, but back when I was a teenager, I would get fighting mad over any insinuation that I was an Indian.

When I married, my husband managed to keep my temper active. There was a love song in those days called "The Kickapoo Indian Maid." He constantly teased me, calling me his little Kickapoo Indian.

After our marriage, we moved to Dallas, Texas, where my husband managed a Star Cash grocery store in the largest chain grocery company in the city. One day he introduced me to his friend, Dr. Hobby, who was a brother to the Texas governor at that time, Governor Hobby. Forrest had been telling me about this prominent man, but when he introduced me by saying, "Meet my Kickapoo Indian," I was humiliated and angered almost beyond endurance. Right when I wanted to be dignified! I was upset, and I guess it showed. Doctor Hobby was amused at my frustration, so he joined the ranks of my teasers.

Doctor Hobby was a bachelor and lived above a drugstore across the street from the store Forrest managed. Not having a family, he must have been lonely, for he visited the store quite often. He became an especially close friend when I became very sick during the great flu epidemic not long after our marriage. Even after my recovery a cough lingered and nothing seemed to help. Dr. Belma, the family's trusted physician, exhausted his remedies without success.

My mother learned of the situation and sent me a prescription that had been handed down through her family for years. Both her parents and her brother, Jake, were doctors. When she sent it to me she told me I would have to have a doctor's help to get it filled. Dr. Hobby gladly offered his help, an act that seemed to cement our friendship. I recovered quickly from that ailment.

Though I highly respected the man, I could not endure the humiliation when he joined my husband in teasing me about my Indian blood. Especially in the presence of strangers.

Dr. Hobby loved to say, "Look, Forrest, at Oma's beautiful olive complexion, her high cheekbones, and that gorgeous, long, black hair! Anyone can plainly see she is an Indian!" His flattery in no way could prevent me from venting my uncontrolled temper. My furious response always amused them, so the teasing went on constantly. When I was born again, God gave me victory over my outbursts of temper, and even the teasing didn't rile me any longer. That took the fun out of it, so the teasing died away.

The most important thing to me today is, not my Indian blood, but the blood of my Savior. When I was born again I became a new creature. Old things passed away and all things became new. A lot of people lightly use that expression "born again," but their lives do not prove and the Bible does not support their claim.

We know Jesus taught, "Except a man be born again, he cannot see the kingdom of God" (John 3:3). He also said, "Except a man be born of water and of the Spirit, he cannot enter into the kingdom of God" (John 3:5). When a person is baptized in water in Jesus' name, he is born of water, and when he is filled with the Holy Ghost he is born of the Spirit. That is why Peter, who was one of the twelve disciples whom Jesus had taught for three and a half years concerning the establishment of the New Testament church, said, "Repent, and be baptized every one of you in the name of Jesus Christ for the remission of sins, and ye shall receive the gift of the Holy Ghost" (Acts 2:38). The Lord had given the same apostle Peter the keys to the kingdom (Matthew 16:18-19). And Peter unlocked the door to all nations on the Day of Pentecost. (See Acts 2:5.)

The blood of Jesus was shed for our sins. Regardless of whether we have Indian blood, Chinese blood, Irish blood, or whatever, it is essential to have the blood of Jesus applied to our sins. He said, "I am the way, the truth, and the life" (John 14:6). He also said, "I am the light of the world" (John 8:12). "Walk while ye have light, lest darkness come upon you. . . . While ye have light, believe in the light" (John 12:35-36).

A born-again person, therefore, is someone who has obeyed Acts 2:38. He has truly repented and been baptized in the name of Jesus, as well as been filled with the Holy Ghost. He has put on the Lord Jesus Christ (Romans 13:14); therefore he makes no more excuses for his flesh. By the Spirit of Jesus Christ he has power to overcome the "works of the flesh" such as wrath and strife, for those who do these works of the flesh "shall not inherit the kingdom of God" (Galatians 5:19-21).

Father and I looked more like Indians than anybody else in our family. Yet looks alone could not help us get in on the program of giving Oklahoma land to Indians. Neither will just saying, "I am a born-again Christian" get people into the kingdom of God. We must be truly born again, which comes by obeying God's Word. Psalm 87:6 says, "The LORD shall count, when he writeth up the people, that this man was born there [Zion]." The Scripture also says, "If we walk in the light, as he [God] is in the light . . . the blood of Jesus Christ his Son cleanseth us from all sin" (I John 1:7). We do not have the blood of Christ in earthly vessels, like the blood of animals that the priests sprinkled upon people, but the blood of Christ is applied to our lives for remission of sins as we repent and are baptized in the name of Jesus. And through His blood we receive the Holy Ghost!

The Acts 2:38 message and experience was instituted by Jesus Christ Himself and proclaimed by His apostles. Only the light of God's Word will show us the way to eternal life. Only as we walk in all the light that God shines upon our path can we be saved.

It was said that my Grandfather Harris was in some way related to Cynthia Ann Parker, as cousins, the best I remember. It is also rumored that Cherokee Indian blood was in the Francis side of my family. I have no way of knowing just where I inherited my Indian blood, but thank God, I fully understand how the blood of Jesus Christ has washed away my sins and made me a part of the family of God!

Forrest Ellis, Oma's husband, at first store managed for Star Cash Co. around 1917.

$\mathcal{M}$Y $\mathcal{I}$NHERITANCE

One thing was different about the congregation I faced in Sherman, Texas, back in 1944: many of them were my relatives! My heart raced with gladness, but my nerves kept pace with apprehension, knowing I would have to preach in the presence of these loved ones. I recognized my Uncle Henry's widow, Aunt Annie Francis, seated beside her brother and his wife. They represented my father's side of the family. Next to them were descendants of my Grandpa Harris: his youngest son, Jack, with two of his children, Lucy and Andrew.

I could not really gauge their reception to the service there in that Jesus Name Pentecostal church, but when I gave an altar call following the message all three of my Harris relatives came forward and sought God. Not only that, they returned every night! Sickness prevented Uncle Jack from attending one night, so after service I went home with my cousins Lucy and Andrew to check on their father, since they were still living at home at that time. Imagine my thrill and surprise when Uncle Jack informed us he had been filled with the Holy Ghost, speaking in tongues, as he prayed alone that night!

Conspicuous by his absence was another relative who lived in that city, my Uncle Andrew Ladd. He had married my father's sister, Joann Francis. I often heard my parents and my dad's brother Bob, who lived with us, refer to my Aunt Jo and Uncle Andrew. Both my father and Uncle Bob had received an endowment from Grandpa Francis's estate when they left home to make a place in this life for themselves.

Not so with Andrew Ladd, the man who married their sister. He was an orphan. One remark in particular left a deep impression upon me as a child. They said, referring to Uncle Andrew, "We will have to say that he lifted himself up by his own bootstrap." They were surprised, without malice, when this orphan boy surmounted his handicap of poverty and achieved success. By the time I was grown Uncle Andrew Ladd was a wealthy financier.

Uncle Andrew did come to visit me while I was ministering in Sherman, Texas. Of course, he did not come to the church, because he was a strict member of a church that completely rejects the Pentecostal experience today. I was acquainted with this type of treatment, as most of my father's relatives were of the same belief and would have nothing to do with Holiness churches. But Uncle Andrew did come one day. He asked me to take a car ride with him. As we rode toward the business district of the city, he explained that he had some things he wanted to show me. When he parked at the courthouse square, he began to point out building after building that he owned, renting them to companies, offices, and various businesses. In addition to all this, he explained that he owned numerous homes all over Sherman and farms scattered around the countryside. All of these were rented and producing a tremendous income.

"During the Depression, Oma," my uncle confided, "my family felt no ill effects. And today I have greater wealth than I had then. All of this will be an inheritance for my son and daughter. They will be able to live sumptuously." Pausing to allow these facts to register and judging that I was properly impressed, he lowered his voice and said sincerely, "Oma! What kind of inheritance are you leaving your children?"

At that time I was separated from my husband and my way of living was meager, yet I was so happy to have a chance to tell Uncle Andrew about my rich spiritual inheritance that I prayerfully hoped to pass on to my children and my children's children.

"Uncle Andrew," I answered, "when it comes to this world's goods I do not possess a dime's worth of anything. I own a cardboard suitcase with a few changes of inexpensive clothing. However, I did inherit a great legacy from my Grandfather Harris, who died back in 1899. If my children also accept it, as I did, we will be exceedingly rich. You see, it is an eternal inheritance. Christ purchased it for all who obey Him (Hebrews 5:9; 9:14-15). Peter called it 'an inheritance . . . reserved in heaven' (I Peter 1:4). When a person obeys the gospel message (I Corinthians 15:1-4) by being baptized in the name of Jesus Christ and being filled with the Holy Ghost (Acts 2:38), he receives the 'Spirit of promise, which is the earnest of our inheritance' (Ephesians 1:13-14). In John 3:3-7 Jesus said, 'Ye must be born again.' Our inheritance will be 'everlasting life,' according to Matthew 19:28-29.

To me, that is the greatest inheritance of all!"

Uncle Andrew Ladd had nothing to reply. He had already lost his wife and one son, and he was getting on in years himself. I'm sure he considered my answer a pitiable reply in the face of his monumental success in this life, but instead of cringing before him I actually felt a pity for him.

To those who read this book, I say, "Those who have inherited great wealth in this life will not be able to take even a penny with them when they leave this world. Only those to whom God has willed an 'eternal inheritance' shall enjoy 'everlasting life' beyond the grave."

My Spiritual Roots

As I have pointed back to my personal ancestry, I want to also direct attention to my spiritual ancestry. I have done quite a bit of research into my family lineage since I was born again as a child of God and became a descendant of faithful Abraham.

In spite of the development of the Roman Catholic Church and the subsequent emergence of the Protestant movement, true Apostolic believers do not count these denominations as the beginning of our spiritual foundation. Instead, we point all the way back to the prayer meeting that Jesus instigated after His resurrection and just before His ascension. He told His followers to wait in Jerusalem for the promise of the Father. He said, "Ye shall be baptized with the Holy Ghost not many days hence." (See Acts 1:1-5.)

By using the Bible, especially the Book of Acts, which is the history book of the New Testament, it is easy to determine the historical sequence of the family of God in this gospel age. A great multitude heard Jesus announce that prayer meeting, but only 120 obeyed. Ten days later "they were all filled with the Holy Ghost, and began to speak with other tongues, as the Spirit gave them utterance" (Acts 2:4).

People out of many nations witnessed this birth of the New Testament church. Peter preached the first Holy Ghost message, which convicted many. When they cried, "What shall we do?" Peter answered, "Repent, and be baptized every one of you in the name of Jesus Christ for the remission of sins, and ye shall receive the gift of the Holy Ghost" (Acts 2:38).

From that day on believers preached repentance, baptism in the name of Jesus, and receiving the Spirit with the sign of speaking in tongues. But false teachers crept in and began to distort the message of the apostles.

My studies identified one of these distortions as the trinitarian doctrine of the Godhead, which was introduced in the A.D. 200s by a man named Tertullian. The Nicene Council of A.D. 325 officially accepted this doctrine, at least in part, for the first time, and it became a fundamental dogma of Roman Catholicism. When Emperor Constantine embraced Christianity, Rome became the chief city of Christianity. As Rome declined in political power, the bishop of Rome, later known as the pope, increased in power.

During widespread confusion and conflicts of governments the Roman Catholic Church became the unifying factor. During this time it sought to force everyone to abide by its creed. Much of the religious belief of the time consisted of human commandments fortified with rituals adapted from pagan religions. Those who objected often became martyrs. It was indeed a very dark day for those who clung to Apostolic truth!

In the 1400s and 1500s a light began to emerge upon Europe. People began to search for the old ways. Men like Erasmus and John Huss lifted their voices for truth. The invention of the printing press brought the Bible into the hands of the people.

In 1517 a German monk named Martin Luther defied the authority of the Roman church by nailing ninety-five objections to the door of a church in Wittenburg, Germany. History labels him as the father of the Protestant Reformation. People such as Calvin, Zwingli, and Wesley saw more and more light in the Word of God. Many denominations now point to one or another of these men as their founding fathers.

But not so the Apostolics. They insist on pointing all the way back to the Day of Pentecost as their origin. Thus they are also called Pentecostals.

At the turn of the twentieth century, the Pentecostal experience fell afresh in the city of Topeka, Kansas. The message of the Apostles had survived the Dark Ages, the Reformation, and denominationalism. The message Peter preached on the Day of Pentecost was proclaimed afresh.

In the year 1898 my parents were married. In 1900 Charles F. Parham and his wife opened a Bible study and prayer home in Topeka, Kansas. The house they rented was called Stone's Folly because it was a project started very grandly by a man named Stone and left unfinished for lack of finances. There was an observation tower on the property that was used for prayer.

On January 1, 1901, the Holy Ghost fell in a prayer meeting there. Agnes Ozman asked Parham to lay hands upon her head as the Bible recorded the apostles had done. As Parham prayed for her to receive the Holy Ghost, her face lit up and she began to speak with other tongues. The Parhams and many others soon shared the same experience. A Topeka newspaper said, "The devotees in Parham's Bible School claim the recovery of that which was lost." In a few years the latter-day Pentecostal revival captured widespread attention and spread around the world, especially through the Azusa Street Mission in Los Angeles under William Seymour.

Gimpers

The word *gimper* cannot be found in Webster's dictionary. It may have been coined by Dr. M. R. DeHaan, the Radio Bible Class teacher, and Charles Swindoll, author of a best-selling book, *Growing Strong in the Seasons of Life*. In defining the word, Swindoll said, "Gimpers never run in packs, they're loners. A gimper is just one of a kind." As examples he named Moshe Dyan, a gimper in Israel's Six Day War; Susanna Wesley, a gimper of motherhood; Abraham Lincoln, a gimper president; and Thomas Edison, a gimper inventor.

To this prestigious list I feel I could add the name of my grandfather, Andrew Jackson Harris. He truly stood alone when he embraced the Holiness doctrine. The Francis and the Harris families totalled twenty-four (each family had ten children.) All belonged to the Churches of Christ except Grandfather Harris.

On the spiritual side of my ancestry I would have to list Abraham, the father of the faithful, as a gimper.

God's people are gimpers. There is none like God's people, "even like Israel" (II Samuel 7:23-24). They are

"The holy people, The redeemed of the LORD" (Isaiah 62:12), "an holy nation, a peculiar people, . . . which in time past were not a people, but are now the people of God" (I Peter 2:9-10). Spiritual Israel, Abraham's heavenly seed of promise, of which I am a family member by the new birth, was once a people of fleshly lusts, but now we are a people separated from sin, and we are to cleanse ourselves "from all filthiness of the flesh and spirit, perfecting holiness in the fear of God" (Romans 15:16; II Corinthians 7:1).

My Spiritual Inheritance

God chose Abraham and Sarah as parents of His chosen people. He said, "Abraham shall surely become a great and mighty nation, and all the nations of the earth shall be blessed in him" (Genesis 18:18). God had a reason for choosing this certain couple. The Scripture says, "For I know him, that he will command his children and his household after him, and they shall keep the way of the LORD, to do justice and judgment; that the LORD may bring upon Abraham that which he hath spoken of him" (Genesis 18:19).

According to Galatians 3:14 and 29 the New Testament church inherits the spiritual promises given to Abraham: "That the blessing of Abraham might come on the Gentiles through Jesus Christ; that we might receive the promise of the Spirit through faith. . . . If ye be Christ's, then are ye Abraham's seed, and heirs according to the promise."

As we receive this great inheritance, we must also pass it on to our children. The Bible says, "Train up a child in the way he should go: and when he is old, he will not depart from it" (Proverbs 22:6). It is my old-fashioned opinion that children should not merely be told what to do; they should be trained to obey.

Pentecostal mothers have a tremendous job of exercising law in the home. Proverbs 6:20-23 says, "My son, keep thy father's commandment, and forsake not the law of thy mother. . . . For the commandment is a lamp; and the law is light; and reproofs of instruction are the way of life."

In my childhood home my father made the commands, and Mother forced us to obey them. She was the law of our home. Father often made commands regarding the housekeeping in our home. He read a great deal, so clean lamps were important to him. There were six rooms in our home, with a kerosene lamp in each room. The lamps had a clear glass globe that had to be washed and polished. Some nights while Dad was reading, candle flies would fall into the globe, and those burnt flies would smoke the globe. He would say to Mother, "Be sure to have the girls clean the lamps tomorrow." I can assure you, Mother did just that! Her law was kept well in our home.

If we wait for our children to receive a Holy Ghost experience to guide them it may be too late. Character may be twisted and warped while we wait. The shaping and molding of character is a tremendous responsibility!

Allow me to make the comparison of a child's character and a young tree sapling. In 1980, a tornado in Grand Island, Nebraska, uprooted and destroyed all the trees around our home. I went to the nursery and purchased young fruit trees to replace them. Later, during a wind storm, I looked out the window and saw my young pear tree at the northwest corner of the house being whipped in every direction. Remembering that the old tree which had stood at the southeast corner had been twisted and crooked even though the trunk was at least two feet in diameter, I determined not to allow that young pear tree to become like the old tree. I hired a man to do as the nursery manual instructed. He anchored my tree with training guide ropes in every direction. And in the Bible we have a training manual for rearing children!

Hear the instruction of an old soldier of the Cross who has almost finished her course: Pentecostal, Holiness parents must train their families to look like Holiness people. A godly appearance is a badge of identity before the world. Our daughters must dress decently, use no makeup, and never cut any part of their hair. Our sons should always have a neat haircut and dress as gentlemen. Genesis 18:19 teaches parents to command their children to "keep the way of the LORD." Holiness is such a wonderful part of our spiritual heritage that I feel an urgency to remind my own descendants and Apostolic believers everywhere to hold fast to this great legacy.

In closing this chapter regarding my inheritance and my spiritual roots, I want to share a conversation I had with my mother shortly before her death. Mother did not believe in women preachers. She thought I was a gimper, one of a kind. But I differed with my mother. She said, "Oma, the Scriptures do not teach that God called women to minister His Word. But I do believe God intended for you to minister, for you were such an unusual child. The Lord seems to have motivated and directed you into a miraculous life."

"Mother," I answered, "there is no respect of persons with God (Romans 2:11). The Lord would never have used me to preach His Word if it had not been in His plan to call His handmaidens to prophesy (preach) as in Acts 2:17-18. Neither would I have preached if God had not confirmed my call with signs following as in Mark 16:20: 'They went forth and preached everywhere, the Lord working with them, and confirming the Word with signs following.'"

Since the Day of Pentecost God has been pouring out His Spirit upon both men and women. Those who are called to preach and teach must do so with diligence.

My Grandfather Harris was a Holiness gimper. Proverbs 13:22 says, "A good man leaveth an inheritance of his children's children."

Uncle Jack's daughter, Lucy age 17.

PART TWO

$\mathscr{M}$OTHER'S $\mathscr{P}$RAYERS

The earliest adventure of my life I cannot rehearse as an eyewitness account. The reason? I was too young. My mother was the heroine of the story, so her version is the only information available. She always prefaced her telling of the story with thankfulness for being taught and trained to pray by her father, my Grandfather Harris.

When my parents married in 1898, they moved from Texas to a place called Cliff in the Indian Territory, now known as Oklahoma. They took my father's brother Bob with them. There was no law force in the area, so it was a refuge for Indians and outlaws who would cross over the Red River into Texas to raid, murder, and steal, then escape back into the Territory.

When my parents went to Cliff very few people were trying to pioneer in that wild and untamed country. The shanty they moved into was many miles from neighbors. A trip to the nearest town to buy supplies took more than a day. The family who gave up the house before my family occupied it said, "We are going back to civilization!"

In 1899, when I was only two weeks old, Mother related that it came time for Dad and Bob to go for supplies. They did this only twice a year because of the great distance. Mother was unused to being alone, being the youngest of ten children before her marriage.

The men arose and departed by 4:00 A.M. that fateful day. Mother was petrified with fear but managed to fill in the day with extra chores. Darkness was an altogether different story. In the front yard of this house was a grave of a woman who died before the use of public cemeteries. The grave was marked with a tombstone, a full-size image of a woman dressed in white.

Mother knew the men would not be back before 2:00 A.M. She made it fine until around midnight. Suddenly eerie screams filled the night. They sounded like a woman screaming in fear. My mother leaped from the bed and ran to the front window of the house. Peering into the darkness of the front yard she saw only the moonlit tombstone, now totally transformed as the screams emanated from it. As my mother watched in horror, trembling and quaking with fright, she saw a panther step from behind the stone.

Immediately, Mother remembered having heard that a panther's scream is similar to a woman's screaming. She knew she had nothing to fear from a ghost, but with the knowledge came a greater terror. She also remembered old wives' tales that a panther could smell the scent of a newborn baby and would make attempts to devour it.

Before her horrified gaze the panther began to stalk around the ramshackle house. In Mother's estimation it was searching for a place to break in and make her two-week-old baby its prey. My mother often repeated her reaction to this danger. She would say, "It was then and there I began to put into practice the lessons on prayer that my father had taught me."

My grandfather's instructions had been specific. He taught, "When trouble comes, put your trust in God. When you call to Him in faith, He will hear."

Mother felt if that panther half tried it could have gained entry into that poorly built house. But in her hour of desperation she called on the Lord, and years later she told me emphatically, "Oma, I believe God heard my prayer that night and saved you from that panther!"

Thus the legacy of prayer was passed from father to daughter, and then to her daughter. I have always treasured this inheritance.

In October of 1978, shortly before she died, my cousin Winnie Spurgeon Jones, one of my Grandfather Harris's granddaughters, told us a little more about our grandfather's prayer influence. Listening was my brother, Jesse Francis, his son Richard, and I.

She referred to him by our favorite title. "Grandpop, when he knew he was dying, sent for my parents to come and take over his household. At that time Grandpop had two children he had taken in after the death of his widowed brother. Both of them had whooping cough. When my parents [Minty and Will Spurgeon] learned of it, my mother refused to come because she feared her baby would take the whooping cough. It was often fatal to delicate children and her baby, Lizzie, was in poor health. Grandpop urged them to come anyway and he would pray about the whooping cough threat. He told us he really needed us and he believed God would protect us. Sure enough, we did not have it then, nor any other time throughout our lives."

One thing she also remembered was the way Grandfather spent his time in prayer and service for others. His prayer influence was credited for another one of Grandma Harris's adventures.

She said, "After we quit living in forts and most of the Indians were on reservations, we women enjoyed a freedom we had never known: we could go visiting and shopping! We had to use wagons drawn by oxen because there was a shortage of horses. One day we decided to visit our neighbors. Usually, the oxen were lazy and we had to prod them continually to keep them going. Sometimes we used the whip. But that day the horseflies were very bad.

"These flies are called by different names—heelflies, stockflies, or horseflies—not to be confused with the common housefly. Horseflies are large gray flies that draw blood when they bite, and the bite is very painful. When they bite an animal's heels or belly where its tail cannot reach to brush them off, they have been known to drive it crazy unless the brute can find sufficient water to find relief.

"On that day the flies were so bad our oxen became crazed. The old cart was heavily laden with several of the children. I was holding the reins when we came within a half mile of a large pond. When those oxen smelled that water they just took off running across gullies and bushes, down one incline and up another, not sidestepping anything in their way. Every moment seemed as if the cart would roll over or we would be flipped out of it. All our Gee commands, all our Haw commands, and even our Whoa commands had no effect. We could only hold on with all our might and pray. The oxen did not stop until they were in deep water. By the grace of God none of us were injured."

As grandmother finished her story she would remind us of grandfather's admonition: "When in trouble or in danger, always pray."

These stories about Grandfather's prayer instructions were a constant part of my childhood. They have played a decisive part of my life. I am praying that Grandfather's prayers will continue to affect my descendants after I am gone from this life. I have added my prayers to his and the purpose of my books has been to influence people to use the weapon of prayer. My grandfather prayed. He taught my mother to pray, she taught me to pray, and I have endeavored to recommend prayer to all who would hear me.

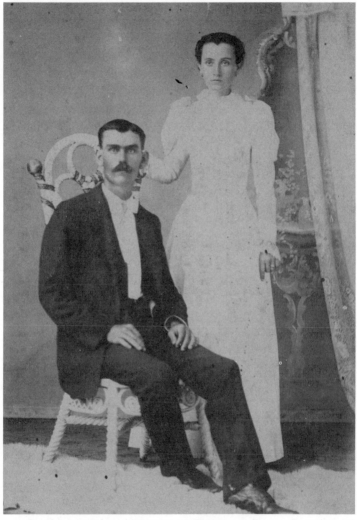

Oma's parents' wedding picture, Thomas Jefferson Francis, and Nicey Pairlee Harris.

$\mathcal{L}$ESSONS ON $\mathcal{D}$ISOBEDIENCE
AND $\mathcal{L}$YING

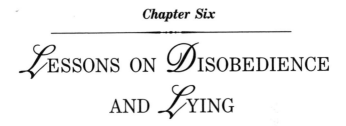

By the time I was four years old I was well aware of my father's expectation that I be perfect in obedience and tell the truth at all times. Lying and disobedience were sins that my father taught me would prevent me from going to heaven. He and my mother certainly put the fear of God in me. I did not always appreciate it, but now in my old age I am able to look back upon it as valuable character-building instruction.

By the year of 1903 my parents and Uncle Bob had built several buildings on ranch and farm land in the Indian territory joining the Texas Panhandle. Several families had also settled nearby and formed a small village called Carl. It was soon a prosperous community. My father, a young Church of Christ minister, established a church group that met in the community school house. There I attended every Sunday and received much valuable instruction in basic Bible knowledge and the building of upright character. I am so thankful I had such teachings while I was still young and tender in heart.

Even though my father was harsh and seemed to be cruel with his discipline at times, I am sure he did not mean to be brutal. He was so intent upon teaching us to be obedient he often did not realize that he used his strong hands too heavily upon his young children.

Many times his younger brother would come to our rescue. The two men were very different in temperament. Daddy was very quick tempered, overbearing, and somewhat cruel when provoked. Uncle Bob was the exact opposite: very gentle, kind, and understanding.

The Cottonseed Pile

The first major lesson of my lifetime concerned disobedience and lying. Even though I was only four years old, I learned the lesson well enough to last a lifetime.

One morning father said, "Oma, you and Bill must not go near the cottonseed bin in the barn. I have put some special, improved seed in the bin for my next planting. I have the cottonseed nicely rounded in a pile and it is important that it is not trampled down, for that would ruin it. Do you understand?"

"Yes, sir," my smaller brother, Bill, and I both murmured. The thought of going in that barn never entered our minds. When Papa put something off limits, we knew it was OFF LIMITS.

At noon that day the men came in for lunch. Daddy ambled over to the barn and then came rushing toward the house yelling, "Oma! Bill! Come to me this minute!"

Bill and I could tell by the tone of his voice that we were in big trouble. But we didn't know what we had done. Daddy sounded fighting mad.

Trembling and fearful, we approached our father. Our fear was of him, not any wrong we may have done. He mistook our hesitancy to be guilt.

"Which one of you has been playing in my cottonseed bin?" he roared.

"Not me, Papa!" said Bill.

"Not me, Papa!" I answered.

"Somebody is LYING! You know you have strictly been taught never to tell a lie. Now you have committed two very serious sins: first you have disobeyed your father and now you have lied to cover your sin!"

Bill, being so young, and knowing he had not committed the deed figured quickly who must have been the guilty one and answered firmly, "Oma did it!"

My father believed my brother because I was older and usually was the instigator of most of our transgressions of his rules.

Without another word he grabbed me and whipped me soundly. Then he asked me to confess my sins. Knowing I had not done it I felt a confession would be a lie and I dared not tell a lie! My refusal merited another whipping. Still I would not say that I had disobeyed and told a lie. He interpreted my clinging to the truth as stubborness and punished me over and over, each time becoming more severe. Mother began to plead with him to spare me, but he was provoked beyond reason.

The commotion inside the house attracted Uncle Bob's attention in the barn. He came running. Arriving on the scene, he had no idea what had caused the disturbance but he was appalled at the judgment my father was administering. "Tom!" he cried, "stop beating that child right now!" He punctuated his comment by jerking me from my father's grasp and encircling me with his arms.

So distraught was my father that he glared at Uncle Bob and proceeded to try to wrest me from his embrace. Daddy cried, "Leave me alone! She lied to me after tearing down my cottonseed! No child of mine—"

"NO!" Uncle Bob interrupted. "She did not lie. I tore down that seed pile!"

The shock of his statement was almost like a physical blow to my father. He staggered back as Uncle Bob continued to explain, "I sold some of that cottonseed to Tom Hyatt after you left for the field this morning. I did not have time to pile it back up so I put it off until this evening."

I can't even remember how father reacted after that. But the realization of how firmly he believed in obedience and truth was indelibly imprinted upon my heart. I have come to appreciate this training because I was also taught to fear God, and these lessons have served to keep me in the path of righteousness.

I learned another lesson that day besides the one about the importance of obedience and telling the truth. Uncle Bob's actions as my rescuer helped me to better understand Jesus as my Savior.

Uncle Bob came to my rescue about two years later when I came into conflict with Papa's obedience rules again. This time I really was a transgressor.

Watery Grave

Once a year we had a cat killing at our house. Cats were important to us because we stored a lot of grain in our barns and we kept cats around to keep down the rat and mouse population. The problem was, the cats multiplied too. Cats are really nice pets, which Bill and I learned. We could tame even the wildest of them. Of course, this made them want to come to the house to be near us. My parents could not bear cats at the house. So once a year Uncle Bob and Papa would thin out the older cats and kill them.

On the night before cat-killing day, when I was six years old, Grandma George, an elderly woman who was a member of my daddy's church, came visiting. Years before she and her family had come to America by boat from Ireland. She had married, but after the death of her husband she was a lonely old lady. Often she came and spent several days. We didn't mind because she was full of stories, and we loved to hear her rehearse the events of her lifetime.

The crickets were chirping outside as we sat in rapt attention to Grandma George. She told about a man who died on their sea voyage from Ireland. They put him in a box and dropped him into the sea. A few days later when they landed in America, they were surprised to find that the box had washed up on shore. When they pried open the lid they were astonished to find him well preserved.

"The ocean water must have helped keep him looking so natural," she surmised. Therefore they were able to give him a proper burial.

We were rushed off to bed knowing that tomorrow was cat-killing day and we had a part to play. We children had to dispose of the dead bodies. Actually, we dreaded the events of the next day, for many of those cats were our personal pets. We hated to give them up, but we dared not say one word.

After Daddy and our uncle had performed their duties as executioners, Daddy commanded Bill and I to get our little wagon and gather up the dead cats. "Haul them across the cow pasture and throw them into the canyon," he demanded.

It was a sad little funeral procession that bounced across the fields that day. As we neared the pond where the range stock watered, inspiration struck me.

"Remember the man who lasted longer in the water?" I challenged Bill.

"What do you mean?" Bill queried, knowing I was referring to Grandma George's story from the night before.

"Well, why couldn't we put our cats in the pond water, and they'll last longer, and we can come see them every day and . . ."

"That's a good idea!" replied Bill. "How can we do it?"

"Don't you have some kite string in your pocket?" I asked.

"Sure," said Bill. "How much do you need?"

"Enough to tie around each cat's leg, then reach to a wooden stake we will pound into the ground. That way they can't float away!"

In short order the deed was done. We did not consider that we were disobeying father, for we had disposed of the cats. Papa and Uncle Bob had created the pond themselves, building up a dike to dam up a spring. It formed a large basin of water for our stock at a time when there was a real water shortage and other farmers were losing cattle. The stakes we drove in the dam to tie our cats weren't even noticeable.

Several days later when Uncle Bob and Father came in at noon for lunch they were greeted by a most unusual sight. A large number of cows were standing beside the barn.

"Tom," exclaimed Bob, "those cows have their tongues all lolled out as if they are starving for water! Do you suppose the pond has gone dry?"

"If it is we are in for serious trouble," my father answered. "I have heard that several springs have dried up in the vicinity."

"Well, let's go ahead and eat lunch," Uncle Bob said. "Afterwards I'll jump on old Dutch [his saddle horse] and ride out to investigate."

It was a hot August afternoon. When Bob returned from the pasture our family was lounging on the front porch on pallets trying to catch a breath of air. Uncle dismounted from his horse and came and sat down on the porch steps, beckoning for Bill and me to come to him.

Sensing trouble, Papa stood up and hovered over us as Uncle Bob swept us into his arms. I put my arm around his neck and began to tremble. Though not a word of explanation had been said, I felt doom already in the atmosphere.

Uncle Bob said, "Tom, let me talk to Oma and Bill before you do anything rash!"

"What do you mean? What have they done?" Papa insisted. "I'll give them a whipping they'll never forget. Turn them loose!"

Uncle Bob had a hard time holding my daddy back. He said, "These children are just babies. They are innocent of the harm they have done. They had a reason for their actions, regardless what we older folks think. I intend to find out."

71

"Harm!" Papa repeated, but before he could make further interrogation, Uncle Bob turned to me and asked kindly, "Oma, why did you and Bill lariat those cats in the cow's drinking water?"

Father seemed to go wild.

As young as I was, I sensed that what we had done was very wrong. I was already trembling, but at Daddy's outburst I began to shake terribly. I could hardly speak to answer Uncle Bob's question. At last I was able to whisper, "Grandma George said that a man kept longer in that ocean water. We thought that nice, cool water where the cows drink would keep our poor cats longer and we could go see them every day. We didn't know the cats would keep the cows from drinking." By this time I was weeping uncontrollably. "We don't want the cows to die!" Even now, I can remember the true conviction that gripped my young heart.

"There! You should know, Tom," cried Uncle Bob fervently. "Every one of us heard Grandma's story that night. These children meant no harm!"

We were guilty as charged. We had disobeyed Father, we came to realize. But Uncle Bob became our advocate. I am now past ninety years old, but I shall never forget the day Uncle Bob pleaded our case. In later years it was easy for me to understand how Jesus became my advocate when I was guilty as charged.

Uncle Bob's example of helping me during my childish troubles became a spiritual lesson in later years. Jesus Christ, our Lord and loving, compassionate Savior, gave His life as a ransom and is "the Saviour of the world" (John 4:42). "He is able also to save them to the uttermost that come unto God by Him" (Hebrews 7:25). I have preached about this Savior for more than sixty years. My father's strict teachings helped prepare me for such a vocation. The apostle Paul said to "walk worthy of the vocation wherewith ye are called" (Ephesians 4:1).

Not only did my father not tolerate disobedience and lying, I learned later that neither does the Lord tolerate such sins.

It is not God's will for us to sin, but if we do so, the Bible says, "My little children, these things write I unto you, that ye sin not. And if any man sin, we have an advocate with the Father, Jesus Christ the righteous" (I John 2:1).

Chapter Seven

$\mathcal{E}$YEWITNESS

$\mathbf{E}$ven in the 1990s an eight-year-old would not be allowed inside an operating room. But in 1907, when I was only eight years old, I was an eyewitness to an operation performed on a kitchen table. The story is one I am sure my relatives would insist I leave on record.

First of all, I am thrilled to say, I had a true experience of repentance in the year 1907. A minister who called himself a sanctified Baptist came to our village, called Carl. This was two years after Uncle Bob had been our advocate during the dead cat episode of my childhood. My heart was tender toward the story of Jesus as my Savior. My repentance was real and genuine and a lifelong commitment.

Another member of the congregation had an experience unprecedented in our region. Her name was Mrs. Inlow, and she was the wife of our local doctor. As she earnestly sought the Lord, she suddenly fell over, apparently unconscious. I was an eyewitness of this also. As we began to get concerned about her, she unexpectedly leaped to her feet and began to shout and dance all over the church, speaking in a language we could not understand.

This really alarmed everybody. Some said, "She is talking out of her head." By this they meant she didn't know what she was saying herself. At that time we had no knowledge of the baptism of the Holy Ghost. Years later, after my own Pentecostal experience and sixty years of witnessing people being filled with the Spirit, I can now say her experience was as genuine as any I ever saw.

Later, she told us she had a vision during the time she lay unconscious. At the time people were somewhat skeptical. The day came when those same skeptics acknowledged that the episode must have been a divine preparation for the ordeal she faced.

The Carl General Store was owned by a bachelor named Mr. Job. He also owned a home that he rented to the doctor and his family, reserving a room for himself.

One day my cousins, the children of Jack and Mildred Harris, were playing with the Inlow children near the Carl General Store. Going into the Inlow home, the doctor's six-year-old son entered Mr. Job's bedroom and located his handgun. The village of Carl was so far from a bank the store proprietor kept the weapon to protect his income.

"Lucy!" cried the boy. "Look what I found. A toy gun! Let's play bears! Get down on your knees and be the bear. I'll be the hunter."

My six-year-old cousin got down on her knees and the boy pulled the trigger. Nothing happened.

"Now I'll be the bear," the little boy said. He handed the gun to Lucy and, falling to his knees, said, "Shoot me!"

Lucy carefully took aim. During the transaction the gun's safety catch was apparently disengaged. When she pulled the trigger a bullet hit Doctor Inlow's son over the left eye.

I will never forget that tragic day. To an eight-year-old, the sight of a bullet hole in a child's forehead is a traumatic experience. And more was yet to come.

Adults were quickly summoned. Dr. Inlow himself performed the initial examination and pronounced that the patient had little hope of recovery. In those days there was no such thing as an ambulance or motor vehicles of any kind. The country roads were so rough that fast travel was out of the question.

Uncle Jack, Aunt Minnie, and my mother stood by solemnly as Dr. Inlow traced the bullet's course around the skull. It had veered left as it entered his head, plowing and cracking the skull as it traveled around the side of the cranium.

With the nearest town thirty miles away, Dr. Inlow sadly shook his head and told the assembled adults that the boy's only hope was an immediate operation. Even that would be very uncertain. Standing by his side with wonderful composure was the child's mother. Her calm acceptance of the circumstances amazed everyone who witnessed the episode. I was one of those witnesses. The participants did not notice that I stood just outside the window.

I saw Dr. Inlow spread a clean bedsheet on the kitchen table. Then he lifted the unconscious form of his son onto the improvised operating table. There was no running water in the house, but somebody obtained water and put it on the stove to boil. Dr. Inlow placed chloroform and what few tools he had on the table and asked his wife to assist him. I watched as the wonderful, indwelling Holy Ghost sustained this mother in what must have been a supreme trial. Everyone was praying. I was praying. As far as I can remember that was my first experience with intercessory prayer. And the Lord filled the confines of that small kitchen that day.

Dr. Inlows' son lived to grow up and be a doctor himself!

Twenty-seven years later I met a family from Carl, Oklahoma, while I was evangelizing in California. I asked about the Inlows' son and they told me he was even then training to be a doctor right there on the West Coast.

God used the events of that day in 1907 to stir the hearts of the people greatly. "And we know that all things work together for good to them that love God, to them who are the called according to his purpose" (Romans 8:28).

Among those who marveled at Mrs. Inlow's behavior during that emergency operation was my mother. She and Lizzie George had already repented during the visits of the sanctified preachers, but Mrs. Inlow's amazing experience created a hunger in them and many others for a deeper walk with God.

In a court of law, an eyewitness cannot say, "I think," or "Somebody told me." An eyewitness must faithfully tell what he has seen and heard. I am so glad I was an eyewitness when my own mother was filled with the Spirit. We still didn't know much about it, but at eight years old I probably would not have understood everything if all the facts were known!

This much I do know: one morning Mother and I were praying in the living room. Mother was doing more than just saying her prayers. She was earnestly seeking God. All of a sudden she quit speaking in English and started talking just like Mrs. Inlow had when she "spoke out of her head." I watched as my mother became what we now call "drunk in the Spirit." She continued this way until nearly noon, when she remembered she had to prepare lunch for father and Uncle Bob. As she stood to walk into the kitchen she staggered and wobbled so much she became fearful. Turning to me, she said, "Oma, come with me into the kitchen so that if I should fall on the cookstove you can pull me off."

If you had asked me at the time what happened to my mother I could not have told you. But fifteen years later God filled me with the Holy Ghost with the sign of speaking in tongues, and I ceased to be merely an eyewitness. I became a part of the great family of God.

In the first century this experience of being filled with the Spirit of God came to guide people into truth. It works the same way in the twentieth century! The Bible says, "Howbeit when he, the Spirit of truth, is come, he will guide you into all truth" (John 16:13). Jesus also said, "I am the way, the truth, and the life" (John 14:6). The infilling of the Spirit will certainly lead us to know who Jesus is!

Many of us older ministers repented under people who did not have the full truth of the Apostolic New Testament church. But we walked as the light came to us. Jesus said, "Walk while ye have the light, lest darkness come upon you" (John 12:35).

79

The Inlow tragedy in my childhood was very frightening. But the thing that frightens me even more is the tragedy of a soul who refuses to walk in the light that God allows to shine upon him. Let us take heed! "If therefore the light that is in thee be darkness, how great is that darkness!" (Matthew 6:23).

Oma's mother, Nicey Frances and Uncle Jack Harris her brother. He received the Holy Ghost as recorded in the book.

$\mathcal{S}$NAKES AND $\mathcal{M}$ORE $\mathcal{S}$NAKES

How happy I am that my daddy taught me about snakes! Not only did he prepare me to protect my life and that of others, but I later learned that my adversary, the devil, is likened in the Scriptures to a serpent. I have found that the same safeguards we use against death-dealing reptiles may have a spiritual application when dealing with Satan. When teaching my children and grandchildren and all others, I have used these true stories to illustrate my lessons. Moses said, in Deuteronomy 4:10, "The LORD said unto me, Gather me the people together, and I will make them hear my words, that they may learn to fear me all the days that they shall live upon the earth, and that they may teach their children."

Father solemnly gathered us all around in the old quarters we were occupying and began to teach his children. I really didn't feel like a child any longer, but I was not exempted from the instructions regarding snakes. I had become a teenager the year before in Carl, Oklahoma. Now, as a fourteen-year-old girl, I had moved with my family to a sparsely settled area in South Texas, just below San Antonio.

The year was 1913, and as we had traveled by passenger train I could see very little besides prickly pear cactus. Father and the hired hand traveled by freight car, bringing the household goods and livestock. Somehow, Dad's boxcar was sidetracked in San Antonio, so Mother and we children arrived first.

Mother had located a man with a wagon and team and hired him to take us to the place Father had arranged for us to live until he could build a house on the property he had purchased. It turned out to be the old shanty where Father gave us our snake instructions.

On the way to the old cabin, the man who drove the team of horses had asked my mother if she was familiar with this territory. She told him we had plenty of experience in the Indian Territory but admitted that these surroundings were strange to us.

"Wal, ma'am," he had drawled, "I reckon I better warn you about the rattlesnakes, diamondbacks at that. They are everywhere. This old shack I'm taking you to used to be slave quarters. Been empty a long time. Rattlers seem to infest unoccupied places. I'd be mighty careful, ma'am, 'specially with them younguns."

"Yes, sir," Mama stammered. "Thank you very much."

When Daddy arrived about three hours later, Mama had been quick to tell him what the man had said.

So here we were assembled in the old rickety building, listening to Daddy's stern voice. I can't remember the lecture word for word, but I remember he told us the diamondbacks were almost the color of the ground.

"You will have to be looking for snakes to see them," he said. He told us to watch every step we took. And he admonished us to obey instantly if anybody yelled instructions. "If they say run, you run. Don't ask why. Your immediate action could mean the difference between life and death," he warned.

He told us never to let a snake get away. He showed us how to use a hoe to kill snakes, and we kept hoes everywhere not only for garden and yard work but also for snake killing. "The snake you fail to kill may later kill somebody."

We lived in the old slave place only a few weeks. With great relief we moved to our own property, only to discover the snakes were just as prevalent there. In the first year we lived there we killed more than three hundred rattlesnakes!

A baby boy was born four months after we moved into our new home. My parents named him Thomas Woodrow. We called him Tommy. By the time he was eight months old he could crawl as fast as anyone could walk.

One morning I was making up my bed. I had the door open in my bedroom to let the fresh air inside. The quilt was bulky, so I crawled up on the bed on my knees to reach the far corner. Suddenly my baby brother scooted into the room. He had an empty kitchen matchbox in his hand. He headed straight for the open door. Without hesitation Tommy whirled around so he could crawl down the steps backwards. My first thought was, There could be a snake in that back yard!

He dropped to the ground before I could get off the bed and get to him. When I reached the doorway my greatest fear was realized. Tommy was playfully poking at a huge diamondback rattler with his little empty matchbox. The snake was coiling for a strike. Without a second thought I reached out the doorway, grabbed the baby by his forearm, and jerked him with all my might. I threw him through the doorway, and he landed on the floor with a hard bang.

Only God knows how I was physically able to do such a thing. Though I was fifteen years old, I weighed less than a hundred pounds. I had always been frail because, as was discovered soon after my birth, one valve in my heart had not developed. I was very weak and Tommy was a very heavy little boy. The shock, the fright, and the exertion were almost more than my afflicted heart could endure.

My mother rushed into the room in response to Tommy's terrified scream. "Oma!" she cried, "What are you doing to that baby?"

I clutched my chest as I fell across the bed. "Go see" were the only words I could gasp out. One look at my face and Mother didn't even pick up the wailing baby. She told me later she knew instantly it was another snake. She ran to the door and observed the snake shaking its rattler, signifying it was still on the warpath. With quick dispatch she expertly destroyed it with one of our snake-killing hoes.

I lived in that snake-infested country until I married and moved to Dallas, Texas. In 1920, at the age of twenty-one, I returned to my parents' home just before the birth of my first baby.

About three days before the baby's due date, I started down the three steps at the front door. As I placed my foot on the first step and was in motion to take the next step, my father cried out from behind me, "Jump, Oma, jump! A snake is striking at your legs!"

I had not forgotten my childhood instructions. I looked neither to the right nor left; I simply put every ounce of strength I had into that jump. Though my body was heavy and awkward, I managed to clear all three steps and land on my knees with that large reptile stretched out beside me. It was almost as long as I was. My dad had jumped immediately behind me, yelling, "Run, Oma, run!" As I scrambled away as quickly as possible on my knees, Papa grabbed a nearby hoe and killed the rattlesnake before it could coil again.

We learned, over the years, that Papa's snake lecture was full of truth. Likewise have I learned that if I follow the biblical instructions for dealing with that old serpent, the devil, I will be safe.

I suffered no harm from jumping and crawling in response to my father's instructions. Nor did my unborn child. At this time I am ninety years old and LaJuan, my firstborn, is sixty-nine years old. I have been filled with the Holy Ghost for sixty-six years and LaJuan for fifty-eight years. I treasure my own childhood memories as well as the childhood of my children. I have been protected from snakes—physically and spiritually.

Oma's dad and her youngest brother Tommie.

Chapter Nine

$\mathscr{E}$ARTHQUAKE $\mathscr{M}$EMORIES

October 17, 1989: A day to remember. The media gave continuous coverage. Newspaper headlines screamed the news: "EARTHQUAKE IN SAN FRANCISCO!"

As I read the account, secure in my room in Mitchell, South Dakota, my mind flooded with memories of another earthquake in the same place.

I was seven years old when San Francisco suffered that earlier, devastating quake. The year was 1906. Perhaps the events of that faraway place would not have been so memorable had not a new family arrived in our community of Carl, Oklahoma, soon after the tragedy.

A little new girl was added to my classroom. She, too, was seven years old. Her last name was Maywaltz (I'm unsure of the spelling), and though we were very close my memory fails to produce a first name for her.

In my earlier book *Oma and Angels* I referred to a man in our community whom everybody called Crazy Jim Allen. Jim's father was Mrs. Maywaltz's brother. Mr. Allen rented one of my father's farms. Mrs. Maywaltz lost her husband and several children in the 1906 quake. She and her daughter came to live with her brother and his family after the loss of their loved ones. They repeatedly told the stories of the terrible things they witnessed during the quake and the horrible fire that followed.

The little girl had such a sad countenance that I yearned to help her smile and be happy. I would try to comfort and cheer her when she would talk about losing her brothers and sisters and father. I understood by association with these people that the problem was not only theirs but that thousands had been displaced on that infamous day. Therefore, when I read about displaced people in 1989, a chill of pity settled over me.

My acquaintance with the Maywaltz family is not my only childhood memory of the 1906 San Francisco earthquake.

Seven years after that earthquake my family sold our portion of the property in Oklahoma to my Uncle Bob, and we moved to Liveoak County, near Oakville, Texas. Not long afterward a family named Bargely became our nearest neighbors. Mr. Bargely had a younger brother, George, who lived with him. He and my brother Bill became very close friends.

One year our crops were very poor, so George went away to find work in order to help his brother. He found employment near Corpus Christi, Texas. The farms were fertile there, and it didn't take long to accumulate financial assistance.

When George came home he told one of the most unusual stories I have ever heard.

George Bargely said he had been told that a large family had moved to the place where he was employed shortly after the 1906 earthquake in San Francisco. (I could relate to that because I remembered the Maywaltz family coming to Carl about that time.) The man became a very prosperous farmer.

Later, a man came looking for work. People directed him to this wealthy man because he hired a lot of help for his large farms. In the course of their conversation the newcomer mentioned that he had lost everything in the California earthquake.

"Worst of all," he told the farmer, "I lost my wife and all our children. Afterwards, I met a woman who had lost her husband. She was left with a large family of small children. I was touched by her predicament caused by the quake. She was pathetically struggling, and I was very lonely without my family. I suggested that we get married and I would do my best to care for her and her children. It has been a great struggle, but we are blessed to be alive!"

According to George's account, that prosperous farmer said, "Man, I can identify with you in your great loss and suffering! I, too, was involved in that tragic quake. No one else could possibly understand unless he had lived through the experience. I also lost everything I owned in the quake and fire. Worst of all, my wife and children were killed. Like you, I met a woman with a young family whose husband was killed in the disaster. I asked her to marry me and move to Texas, so here we are. Both of us can certainly sympathize with you. I have a house and a farm where you can care for your family. The rent will be more than reasonable. Bring your family to us."

George Bargely's story did not end there. He went on to relate that when the newcomer returned with his wife, the farmer nearly fainted. He recognized her as his wife he thought had been killed in the earthquake. When he hastily summoned his new wife she was astounded to discover the newcomer was none other than her first husband, also considered dead since the earthquake! The two families had been completely exchanged by the ravages of that tragic day.

In the intervening years more children had been born to both couples. Since they had already worked through their grief it was decided that they would remain as they were. Only, instead of renting the house and farm, the wealthy farmer gave them the property.

When I was a fourteen-year-old girl George's story made such an impression that it sprang afresh to my mind when I read about the 1989 earthquake.

My oldest son, Elton, called a few days after the October 17, 1989 quake. He said, "Mother, would you like to go back and live in California?"

"No," I replied.

"Neither do I," he answered. "I feel Texas is the safest place that can be found to live."

"Remember, son, the Mississippi River Valley is noted for the greatest quake in U.S. history!" I stated.

He hesitated a moment, then firmly declared, "Well, I mean to stay away from California anyway!"

After our conversation I went to prayer. In my talk with the Lord I voiced my feelings about the human instinct to stay away from danger. But my greatest concern was for safety in the life to come. There are only two destinations in the hereafter: heaven or hell. Our eternal abode will be determined by the life we live here on this earth. There can be no adjustments once the spirit has left the body. "In the place [condition] where the tree [man] falleth [dies], there it shall be" (Ecclesiastes 11:3).

Those who hear the Word of God and keep it, or do it, will be blessed. (See Matthew 7:24.) "Be ye doers of the word, and not hearers only, deceiving your own selves" (James 1:22). The doer will be blessed.

The Spirit of God will lead a person into a place of eternal safety, so that he will be hid with Christ in God. (See Colossians 3:3.) Only in this life can a person make his hereafter safe. I hope I have, with this book, encouraged many to prepare for heaven.

PART THREE

$\mathcal{I}$N THE $\mathcal{S}$CHOOL OF $\mathcal{O}$BEDIENCE

Have you ever noticed what's left after you squeeze all the juice from an orange? Nothing but a shell. A shell with white membranes that appear dry and twisted from contact with the juice extractor. It is simply all wrung out. Nothing is left to do but to pitch it in the trash or the disposer.

That seemed to be my predicament when I set out to record the stories that inspired and strengthened me throughout a lifetime of loving and serving God. My first three books, *Oma, Oma Talks about Prayer and Faith,* and *Oma and Angels,* contain most of my real adventures. I poured out the drama and suspense, tears and tragedies, miracles and wonders, visitations and deliverances. The highlights have basically been covered. But as I pondered about what was left to make up the contents of this book, I discovered many treasured memories yet to be recorded for posterity. They may lack the fire and action of the more noteworthy events, but they are the stuff that made up everyday life, sustained me in trials, and molded the characteristics of Christianity in this unworthy vessel.

Some of these stories are brand-new, never-published events; others, of necessity, overlap into well-known periods of my autobiography. I have endeavored earnestly to keep this narrative fresh and nonrepetitve.

Come with me into God's school of obedience. If I thought my father was a disciplinarian, what do you suppose I found out when God got a hold of me? Actually, I learned that strict and swift obedience paid the best dividends!

Floating

My children have Sister Nona Freeman to thank for this story. I was reading a book called *Women's Conference '87* published by Focused Light, when an article by Sister Freeman caught my attention. It was titled, "Meet for the Master." In it she described God's wonderful blessings in her ministry. She stated, "Two different times in my ministry God lifted me up off my feet and let me float while I preached! That surely was nice. I didn't think I'd ever tell anybody about it, but it happened to me twice."

I could identify with her words, for God granted me the same experience. The sensation of being lifted by the power of God and released from the pull of gravity, floating in a rapturous anointing of the Spirit of God, was the most thrilling and glorious experience I ever had!

Dallas, Texas, was the site of this strange occurrence. The C. P. Kilgore family, accompanied by a young man named Claude Johnson, had arrived at Brother Matlock's church for a revival. This was during the period of separation from my family, so I was residing with my brother Bill. I served as Brother Matlock's assistant pastor.

The Kilgores had a little boy named James who was about the age of one of my absent little ones. Only God knows how being able to caress that little boy filled a void in my life! Sister Kilgore and I sat behind the piano, and I gladly helped her with the children while her husband preached. Both of us maintained an attitude of earnest prayer.

This was a period of intense suffering in my life. But when I sold out to God and determined to obey Him, I quickly learned that He knew how to recompense.

One Sunday morning during the revival we had a prayer service before dismissal. Later, Brother Claude Johnson and Brother and Sister Ryan came to Bill's home to find me.

"Sister Oma," Brother Johnson blurted out, "did you know that during prayer after the morning sermon that you were floating in the air up above the altar bench, not touching anything?"

"Yes," I answered, "I had what I thought to be a sensation of floating."

"It was not a sensation," he declared. "You were really floating like dust in the air. I have never seen anything like it!"

Brother and Sister Ryan assured me that they had been sitting on the front pew with Brother Johnson and had witnessed the same thing.

I did not tell them that was not the first time I had felt that sensation, but I had never opened my eyes. Their testimonies were the first evidence that it was a reality. Like Sister Nona, I didn't think I would ever tell it, for fear of being scorned.

In retrospect, I recall that each time (they were few and far between) followed a period of intense prayer. I found solace in studying the Book of Job, the story of a man who suffered greatly in spite of doing everything he knew to the best of his ability. The school of obedience is a school of hard knocks, but thank God, there are roses among the thorns!

At the end of that revival, Brother Matlock said he felt led for me to anoint and pray for the sick. I obeyed and everyone in that long line was instantly "slain" in the Spirit the minute I laid hands on them. Twice more in my ministry this occurred. Some years later I observed a charlatan using a trick to make people fall. I feel like charging fellow believers to pray down thrilling results. Anything less is hypocrisy and disobedience.

Hog-Pen Revival

There was a time in my life when obeying God was exactly opposite to what I wanted to do. God let me know that to stay in His will I would have to leave a comfortable place and face seemingly impossible relocation difficulties.

There were some doctrinal differences between the congregation I was serving and me. The circumstances seemed to be leading me away from the truth. When I voiced my determination to obey God and leave, the people scoffed at my ability to do so in my impoverished state during those Depression days, and made some very tempting offers to keep me.

I was almost persuaded to remain. I fought a mighty battle in my mind. "Look," something whispered, "your trailer home is broken down and you have no money to have it fixed. These people will not help you because they don't want you to go. Why not be sensible and remain? You have it made here."

Though young in the Lord I knew the most miserable place to be was out of the will of God. And I was miserable. I began to search for a place to go and soon found an old empty barn not too far away. I told my sixteen-year-old son and the gospel workers with me, "This place could be cleaned up and used as a gospel tabernacle." One end of it had recently been used as a hog pen, but we cleaned that too and built a platform over it.

My son said, "Mama, I think I can repair our trailer enough to drag it these forty miles. We have to have a place to live!" The verse of Scripture came to my mind: "All things work together for good to them that love God, to them who are the called according to his purpose" (Romans 8:28). I believed this verse and stood upon it.

The fact that I felt I was obeying God did not shield me from the critics. "Do you mean you are refusing all we have to offer in favor of a pig pen? Do you think people will respect you in such a place?"

That proved to be one of the wisest moves I ever made in my ministry. God gave us twenty precious souls in that hog-pen revival.

It was during that hog-pen revival that the pastor of the Weedpatch, California, church asked me to preach for him when his new church was finished. I promised to do so. He turned out to be the future grandfather of the yet-to-be-born co-writer of two of my books.

Immediately following the close of the revival in the former pig pen, a California church official, W. L. Stallones, asked me to preach an arbor meeting in a place called Tugglesville, known as Tulare, California, today.

Revival in the Golden State

The years from 1938 to 1940 seemed to be my zenith years. My ministry was very fruitful: seventeen were saved during the arbor meeting, after which Brother Stallones asked me to pastor the little group. The revival continued after the building was erected, and 139 more were born again. During this time I also regained possession of my missing children and fulfilled the promised revival in Weedpatch. There, another 150 were born again—baptized in water and filled with the Spirit. That made a total of 326 souls rescued because of my blind obedience to God! The bonus was that my brother Jesse, my daughter Jackie, and my son W. G. all received the Holy Ghost during that period.

Without Prejudice

The word *obedience* brings to mind a wonderful family in that 1938 congregation. There were ten children when they came, and twins were born later. The parents and some of the children were already filled with the Spirit, but before long the entire family was Holy Ghost–filled except the newborns.

The mother of that precious black family was an outstanding example of Christian motherhood.

It was plain to see the children were taught obedience and manners in the home. The home was kept spotlessly clean. Some people from the Deep South marveled that I would receive tithes of milk and butter from a black family. I quickly informed them that I would rather use food from their home than from some others I knew. I told them, "The Bible teaches me that we should not judge one another by the color of our skin." (There was plenty of prejudice in those days.)

During testimony service one evening, a six-year-old child in the family who had recently received the Holy Ghost stood to his feet. He began to weep and sob as if his little heart would break.

"I am backslidden," he sobbed when he could finally speak. "Today, I cheated my friend when we were playing hopscotch. Please pray for me. I am lost!" Falling to his knees at the altar the child agonized before God for forgiveness.

The child's actions precipitated a mighty move of the Holy Ghost in that service, for many backsliders were present whose hearts were hardened and cold toward God.

Many times we saw the power of God fall when members of this remarkable family would sing. The first time I ever heard "He's Got the Whole World in His Hands" was from a quartet of singers from this beautiful family. When attempting to select the most outstanding family I ever was associated with, my heart bade me bestow the honor on them.

The Desires of Your Heart

I am grateful for many, many things. More than I could ever name. Ranking high on the list would be a blessing I received after the burning of a tent that was part of our living quarters in Tugglesville. Details may be gleaned from one of my other books. I want to repeat it here because I consider it a crowning glory to the multitude of blessings gleaned from the verse of Scripture: "Delight thyself also in the LORD; and he shall give thee the desires of thine heart" (Psalm 37:4).

I stood in stunned attention as that fire consumed everything we owned of any value: musical instruments, keepsakes, linens, clothing. I felt so poverty stricken over the loss of these personal goods, which were really nothing. But they were all we had. We owned such a little but felt such a deep loss.

As the fire raged I had one request, "Lord! There are my pictures! I've saved them all during my life. They can never, never be restored. All else can be replaced if you see fit."

In short order there was nothing left but rubble and ashes.

Fifty years have come and gone since that agonizing trial. And I still say it pays to obey God! We found out soon who were our friends indeed! Our beloved church family from far and near came to our rescue. With Brother Stallones directing the restoration, we actually had more and better things than before.

Among our new possessions were some beautiful new quilts. I learned that Brother Stallones had a large family in his church, the Brokaws, with five sons and three daughters, who were great workers in the church. The mother and daughters and several others had been instrumental in making those quilts and linens. Especially, I remember a set of pillowcases embroidered by twelve-year-old Oma Brokaw.

Many years later, in 1982, I was invited to Gridley, California to preach and introduce my book *Oma*. There I found the pastor's wife, Sister Burl Woodward, was the former Oma Brokaw! They had a beautiful church with a large educational department. How wonderful it was to renew our fellowship and talk about old times. It was so good to see that those children had developed such beautiful characters and were being used by God in His great work. I knew a pair of pillowcases, prepared by loving little hands, had helped to pave the path of service and obedience to God.

Brother Toole was another neighboring pastor who cooperated in Brother Stallones's plans for our new parsonage. It seemed only a short while until we were moving into our brand-new house!

Three weeks after the fire, my son W.G. was digging in the ruins of the fire as twelve-year-old boys will do. I heard him give a joyful whoop.

"Come here, Mama," he cried, "I have found your pictures!"

My pictures.

By His grace I had put that loss behind me. I had even been able to thank God for allowing my loss. Ephesians 5:20 admonishes us to give thanks in all things. Refusing to allow the ashes to renew my grief, I responded to my little boy's summons. He had found the pasteboard box in which my pictures had been stored. As I had expected, the box had disintegrated to ashes as soon as he touched it.

As I approached, he cried, "God has saved your pictures whole!"

It was true. Incredible, unbelievable, but true. There, in a nest of ashes, were my beloved photos. Not one of them had been damaged by the inferno that had claimed everything else!

How does one describe emotion beyond comprehension? God had heard my feeble prayer! Why wouldn't everybody want to serve a God like that?

Chapter Eleven

$\mathscr{D}$ISOBEDIENCE $\mathscr{H}$URTS

That Babylonian garment! It was so beautiful, so soft, so colorful! But it was off limits. Hadn't Joshua instructed that the spoils of this first battle belonged to the Lord? He had said it would be a cursed thing to them if the soldiers took anything for themselves. But, one soldier thought, is it right for him to deprive us in this manner? Here's a wedge of gold! No one will ever know!

The soldier's name was Achan. He disobeyed the divine orders relayed to him from God through his captain, Joshua. He thought no one would ever know. Now everybody knows. His disobedience and subsequent punishment is recorded in the Bible in Joshua 7.

The lust for two things snared him: clothes and money. And the devil hasn't changed his bag of tricks since he duped poor Achan! Disobedience hurts. It hurts the perpetrator and it hurts his family, his associates, and his chances of being saved.

Ask Achan. Israel lost a battle and hundreds were killed the next day because of his disobedience. It drove his captain to his knees. And when judgment was meted out—death by stoning—his wife and children were forced to die with him!

The spiritual parallels are amazing. Number one, Achan laid his hand on the portion that belonged to God, the spoils of the first battle. Afterwards, the warriors were welcome to take the spoils from other battles (Joshua 8). But Achan wasn't there to enjoy them. Do we have any present-day Achans who hold on to God's portion, the tithe?

Number two, clothes and money were his weaknesses. Look around and see if you can find anyone who has failed God today for those same reasons.

Number three, he tried to hide his sins. But he lost out when God told Joshua to get up and get busy because there was sin in the camp. "Be sure your sin will find you out" (Numbers 32:23). When Joshua interviewed the head of every family, Achan couldn't pass the test. When he tried to praise the Lord, Joshua recognized the emptiness of his response. How many heads of families could pass the praise test today? It's strange how the love of money and clothes can make worship empty and hollow.

Last of all, worst of all, it was Achan's fault that his family was killed! Disobedience hurts.

Let me tell you about one of the young ladies who received the Holy Ghost in that Tugglesville revival of 1938. One day she walked into my home wearing riding britches and boots. I asked her to be seated so I could talk to her. I told her I realized she was not aware that Spirit-filled ladies do not wear men's apparel, but the Bible condemns it. Speaking as kindly as I could I explained that she and others had also been wearing their skirts too short. I blamed myself for not getting around to teaching all of my baby saints about holiness. "I will excuse you this time," I concluded, "but after I teach on it I will expect all of you to comply with holiness standards in order to help me on the platform with music and singing."

She said, "Do you mean I can't wear this riding habit again? After paying so much money for it!"

Her response confirmed what I already had suspected; the outfit looked very expensive, in a day when so few had money to buy frivolous things. I considered it dangerous and sinful to go beyond our means and into debt, for the lust of the eyes and the pride of life are condemned in the Bible. I told her so. I told her to read Deuteronomy 22:5.

I remember the look of rebellion that flashed upon her face. She was insulted. I was very troubled by her attitude.

In days to come she continued to wear the riding habit. She was dating a young evangelist from another church. They went horseback riding repeatedly, and she must have shared her opinion of my advice with him.

One Thursday night our church hosted a special youth service for the young people of three churches. We took turns with this weekly attraction for the sake of youthful fellowship. I did not attend. I went to visit the sick and left our youth director, my brother Jesse, in charge.

Brother Stallones was very ill, and I was visiting his home when his young people came there after the service at my church.

"Oh, Sister Ellis!" they cried, "you won't believe what happened tonight. That evangelist from Brother Toole's church who dates one of your young ladies was asked to preach tonight by Brother Jesse. You should have seen the show he put on. He grabbed his belt and lifted his pants toward his armpits, so high his pants were above his socks! He said, 'It's nobody's business what I wear, nor how high I wear my trousers. Nobody is going to tell me what to do!' Oh, Sister Oma, he pranced all over the platform and he looked so disgraceful!''

Brother Stallones gave me a questioning glance. I told him what had transpired and how troubled I had been.

He said, "He will not get away with that behavior. I'll have a talk with that young man. You need help, not hindrance, with all those young saints."

The next day he sent for the young man's pastor to bring him to his bedside. He sharply reprimanded him and threatened to take his credentials if he did not apologize.

Disobedience hurts. Because of one girl's disobedience, she was hurt, I was hurt, her boyfriend was hurt, and a whole lot of young people were hurt. Over clothing.

Makeup and Split Skirts

The saddest stories always end, "If only . . ."

Picture a beautiful Apostolic girl, reared in a United Pentecostal Church, married to a young evangelist. She had musical talent and fantastic singing ability. She devoutly proclaimed her love of souls, her concern for the lost, and her devotion to God, her church, and her husband. Now add a little makeup and a short skirt with a deep split up the back. Watch her as she proudly walks to the piano, exposing her legs as she goes up the steps of the platform.

Add a new pastor to the picture. One who really preaches holiness. Go into the pastor's office and listen as both the pastor and her husband plead with her to give up the makeup and dress more like the Bible teaches. Watch as she shakes her head and walks out. Follow her to a trinitarian church, where she is allowed to do as she pleases and work on the platform.

Now listen to her testimony about loving God, church, and souls. Kind of hollow, isn't it?

All for a little bit of makeup and a split skirt. Clothes again.

This is a true story. If only . . .

I could fill in the names, but I won't. How sad that this situation could be placed in nearly every state in the nation, every city. But it doesn't have to be.

We are not to dress to please ourselves, but to please the One who has called us to be holy as He is holy. "Forasmuch as ye are manifestly declared to be the epistle of Christ ministered by us, written not with ink, but with the Spirit of the living God; not in tables of stone, but in fleshly tables of the heart" (II Corinthians 3:3). An epistle could be defined as a long, formal letter of instructions. Paul sought to establish that born-again believers are living epistles, "known and read of all men" (II Corinthians 3:2). Unbelievers should be able to look at us and see what the Bible teaches: holiness, "without which no man shall see the Lord" (Hebrews 12:14). Only those who live godly will be able to convert a sinner to holiness.

"Love not the world, neither the things that are in the world. If any man love the world, the love of the father is not in him. For all that is in the world, the lust of the flesh, and the lust of the eyes, and the pride of life, is not of the Father, but is of the world" (I John 2:15).

Disobedience hurts.

Misunderstanding the Pentecostals

Sometimes we Pentecostals enjoy a time of swapping amusing stories we all have experienced. Ask my brother, Reverend Jesse Francis, about the time in Vallejo during World War II when a drunk staggered into our service. The power of God was all over the place, and people were dancing and shouting in every aisle and across the platform. The drunk man wobbled around jabbing his finger toward everybody as he attempted to count those rejoicing in the Spirit. He left and soon returned with a large bag. Grinning smugly he began trying to pass out a can of beer to everybody. Jesse told him we didn't need liquor to help us rejoice because our dancing was not the effect of beer or alcohol. The Bible says, "Be not drunk with wine, wherein is excess; but be filled with the Spirit" (Ephesians 5:18).

After this explanation the poor man seemed to be trying to understand the matter when he spied a young lady named Omega Frost kneeling at the altar speaking in tongues very fervently. The drunk approached the altar and stared with amazement at her face. The young sister was totally oblivious to his presence. But the rest of us overheard his comment to her. "Lady," he said, his speech slurred by drunkeness, "you and me have a lot in common: I'm nuts and you're crazy!"

A misconception of Pentecostal behavior is not always humorous. Sometimes it is sad and tragic.

I have witnessed parents who prevented their children from obeying God, to their own sorrow. One such case was a seven-year-old girl from a denominational family who attended one of our services. She came to the altar and was soon speaking in other tongues. Her parents removed her physically from the altar and refused to consider allowing her to return. Presently, the little girl fell ill. Her parents called the doctor, but she asked them to call me.

I arrived just as the doctor was leaving; he told them nothing was seriously wrong with the child. But when we went to prayer the Lord told me the child was dying. I broke the news to the parents as gently as I could. The mother rushed to the little girl's side in time to hear her say, "I am going with Jesus!" She folded her little hands, laid her cheek upon them, gave everyone a beautiful smile, and passed away.

The parents, who claimed to be greatly stirred by this course of events, decided to stay with their prestigious church. They admitted freely that the child had received something special at the Pentecostal altar, but they still could not give up their wealthy and prominent church.

Fern and I wept over this story fifty eight years later. I believe the story could have ended much better if these parents had not disobeyed God.

Disobedience hurts.

Chewing Gum in Church

The car had a Utah license plate. I couldn't imagine who would be visiting us that quiet day in our home in Rapid City, South Dakota. Nor did I recognize the young couple with the infant who made their way to my bedside. When the young father identified himself as Ray Langenegger and went on to ask if I would pray for their eight-month-old son and dedicate him, I must have made the right answers, but my mind was picturing four little boys on Arizona church seats.

World War II was only a couple of years behind us at that time. It was hard to get building materials, but we were determined to have a place to worship God.

Boots and Vivian Langenegger came with their four boys: David, Ray, Bobby, and Billy Joe. What a lively addition to our Sunday school department!

Eventually, we were able to replace our makeshift seating with new seats. I was so protective of our beautiful new church furniture. Very bluntly I made the announcement: "Children, please do not chew gum in church and then park your wads of gum on the bottoms of these new seats."

One Sunday evening as I was preaching I happened to notice the Langenegger boys smiling and winking at each other. I sensed that they were daring each other to initiate the new seats with gum deposits. Pausing in my message, I said, "You boys over there! Take your gum outside, but don't throw it where it can be tramped back in the church!"

Their dad stood quickly and marched his sons from the church. I heard a car door slam. With a sinking feeling, I thought, Oh, no! I have insulted him and driven him away from the church.

I had been working with Brother Boots for a long time to go further than just water baptism. I knew he needed the Holy Ghost. I had observed others who had made the same mistake: they stopped short of the full rebirth. But Jesus signified that it took both water and Spirit to constitute the new birth. (See John 3:3, 5.) As I sometimes say, "This is a know-so salvation. Not guess so, maybe so, or even hope so. You and those around you will hear you speak in other tongues, for that is the Lord's evidence

(Acts 2:4)." God gave utterance to Balaam's mule in Numbers 22:28, so He can surely speak through us!

Though my worry was persistent, I did not see Boots or the boys again that evening. The next morning Sister Langenegger happened to come by my home. I began to apologize for offending her husband.

She cut my remarks short. "Oh, no, Sister Ellis, no way did you make Boots mad. He was upset over the boys' disobedience. You had only recently made that announcement about gum in the church. He started to thrash them outside but decided the uproar would upset both the service and the neighbors. So he took them home and belted every one of them, telling them never to take chewing gum to church again. By the time he quieted their loud crying, got their faces straightened out and washed, and got back to church, service was dismissed. They just picked me up and we drove on back home."

As any pastor would, I appreciated them for training their children to respect the house of God and their pastor.

The Langeneggers were a real help to me when my brother Tommy loaned me the money to buy old army barracks at an auction and we remodeled them for a church and parsonage.

Could it be possible that this young man with his wife and baby from Salt Lake City could be that same little boy who was chewing gum in church? He must not have been offended, either, or he wouldn't have driven all this way to have me dedicate his baby.

Should I mention the gum chewing? He would remember, because disobedience hurts!

Barracks purchased for church in Yuma, Arizona.

Ray Langenegger, wife Sharon and son John visiting Sis. Ellis in Mitchell, South Dakota. John was dedicated in Rapid City when he was 8 months old.

114

Chapter Twelve

ℱACING THE 𝒥UDGE

"Your Honor," I tried to keep the quaver out of my voice, "this woman and her son were near starvation when I took them into my home."

The judge regarded me solemnly.

Nothing I had ever heard about a court of law had prepared me for this day. Sitting on the witness stand and facing the judge was an awesome experience. I was not the one on trial. But well-meaning friends had informed me that there was a possibility I could be jailed for receiving stolen property.

The events leading to this fateful day were simple. I had received a pathetic letter from a lady who had been a member of the church I had pastored ten years before in Clarendon, Texas. Sister Watson informed me that her husband had died and all her children were married except Ivan, her twelve-year-old son. They had settled in Los Angeles to look for work but were destitute and hungry. Could they please come to our home, where she would work as cook and housekeeper for their room and board?

I carried my problem to Brother Stallones, who was very pleased with the prospect. "Sister Oma," he counseled, "you need a consecrated Christian to help you. You have your family and all those young ministers who stay there. The cooking, housekeeping, and the care of the church is such a tremendous load. God knew you needed assistance."

My son Elton and I drove to Los Angeles to move our friends to Tugglesville. While loading their things Sister Watson pointed to two pieces of new furniture and asked if I had space for them in my home. I assured her we could put them to good use since we had very little furnishings for our new parsonage.

Upon our return, a family sent for me to come and pray for their demented father. I rushed to their assistance. The man in question had been a great troublemaker in the church. He constantly made interruptions in the Sunday school lessons. Now he was beside himself and trying to do bodily harm to the family members. We fasted and prayed for days and finally won the victory when the Lord brought a brother I had been asking for to assist me.

Afterward, I wanted nothing more than to get a bath, get something to eat, and go to sleep! Instead, I found my home in an uproar.

Officers from the Los Angeles Police Department had arrested Sister Watson on a charge of stealing the two pieces of new furniture. They had left a summons for me to appear the next morning at 10:00 A.M. for investigation.

Elton and I had to scrape up enough money to make the 165-mile drive immediately. In my extreme fatigue the problem seemed all out of proportion. I could picture the headlines: "Pastor Jailed for Harboring Thief and Stolen Goods."

I simply could not picture Sister Watson as a thief! My family had said she left contending she had not stolen the furniture, so I felt duty bound to do all in my power to stand by her.

My biggest worry was leaving all those baby saints without a leader. Plus, Sister Watson and I both had twelve-year-old sons who needed us. If someone had told me we would be in court soon with those two boys it would have been more than I could have borne.

Sister Watson's trial was a new ordeal for me. She was called on first to testify. I was relieved to hear her explanation of the apparent theft. She told the judge she had been hired to work for the plaintiff but he had not kept his agreement to pay. When she moved she had taken the furniture because she estimated that to be the equivalent of her unpaid wages.

When she told them I had no knowledge of any of those facts, I breathed a sigh of relief.

When it came my turn to testify I was as nervous as if I were the defendant. I gave Sister Watson a good character witness, having been her pastor for some time. Never before had there been any doubt of the Watson family's honesty. They were held in high respect. I told them I was unaware the furniture was not hers, but I was sure she felt justified in taking it in lieu of cash.

The next witness was Sister Watson's employer. He had a good-paying job with the electric power and gas department of the city of Los Angeles. He confessed that he had neglected to pay Sister Watson at the proper time and admitted he had not realized he had missed so many payments.

The judge became visibly angry. He said, "Sir, you are the one who should have been jailed! You have forced this woman and her son to the point of starvation. I order you to make full payment of her wages now, today! Then you may go get your furniture." (God knew we needed money to get back home! The Lord is so compassionate. He cares about our every need.)

Turning to me, the judge said, "Mrs. Ellis, by law this woman should not be set free until the furniture is back in the owner's hands. But considering the facts of this case, I am going to release her now so she can return home with you. That will save you another trip back down here."

What absolute, utter relief! There is something so intimidating about facing the judge. We went on our way rejoicing because we knew there had been an unseen witness in the judge's chamber. He had been our Lawyer in the courtroom, just as so many times He had been our Doctor in the sickroom!

Satan was still determined to bring disgrace upon the Tugglesville church. But thanks be unto God who gives us the victory!

Shortly after the trip to Los Angeles, I looked out over the vineyard outside my kitchen door. I saw just the top of several heads and heard voices. Upon investigation I found it to be Ivan Watson, my son W. G., and several boys I did not know.

"What's going on, boys?" I asked. They all had the same answer: "Nothing."

I questioned W. G. specifically, and he, too, answered in the negative.

"O.K." I concluded, "I feel like something is wrong.

I'll just ask the Lord about it. I'll just ask Him to have the cops put you in jail and nip this in the bud before it goes any farther . . . whatever it is!"

They all looked guilty. I knew the Lord and I were on a hot trail. The Lord moved sooner than I expected, however.

The next morning the sheriff came to my door and informed me that my son and Ivan Watson were in jail. They had been arrested with a gang who had been stealing from a store in Tulare and bringing the merchandise to Tugglesville to bury in the vineyard near my house.

Elton, Sister Watson, and I went to the Tulare jail.

From his cell, W. G. pleaded, "Mama, I told you the truth! Ivan and I did not steal anything. We just didn't tell on the boys when we knew what they were doing."

I told W. G. he had done wrong by not telling. "You are now involved in their unlawful act. We can only ask God to be merciful and help us prove you didn't steal. If you are not guilty, I believe the Lord will help you when you appear before the judge."

Two days later Sister Watson and I were summoned to court again. This time, the judge did most of the talking.

"We have talked with all of these boys and feel we have gotten to the bottom of the matter. Pastor.Ellis, your son has given me the story of his life. I must say I was impressed with his story, especially the progress you made with him in so short a time. I understand you were separated from him when he was two years old. You have had him less than a year now after a period of nearly ten years under the guidance of his grandmother and aunt. When he became quite unruly, I was informed your oldest daughter was of the opinion that you could break him of

119

running away and playing in the streets.

"I asked him how you managed to accomplish that, and he told me you were persistent in sending his older brother out to find him each time he ran away or failed to obey. He said you would take him in the bedroom each time, without fail, and quote the Scriptures to him. He could even repeat some of them, such as, 'Train up a child in the way he should go: and when he is old, he will not depart from it' (Proverbs 22:6) and 'Chasten thy son while there is hope, and let not thy soul spare for his crying' (Proverbs 19:18)."

I could remember another verse I used often in dealing with my children: "Thou shalt beat him with the rod, and deliver his soul from hell" (Proverbs 23:14).

The judge went on to tell me, "You have done the same thing so many times he was able to quote the Scriptures and had done so the last time you took him into the bedroom for a whipping. The boy said, 'She seemed vexed at me and told me she was whipping me to save my soul as well as her own.'"

"Your son also said you gave him a whipping with every ounce of strength you had, then sat down on the bed and cried. He said, 'She said she hated to whip me like that but considered my quoting of the Scriptures as poking fun at her and the Bible.' The boy said, 'Her crying hurt me more than the whipping. So I sat down and put my arms around her and told her not to cry because her whippings didn't really hurt. I told her she couldn't hurt a grasshopper!'"

I remembered the incident as the judge repeated it. I had commended W. G. for minding much better lately, and he had told me he did it because the Bible said so and because I was his mama.

"Lady," the judge was saying, "I wish we had more mothers like you and Mrs. Watson. I would like to ask a favor of you. This is the first time this gang your sons were with have violated the law. Would you please deliver each of these boys to their homes and take the time to tell their parents how you dealt with your son when he would run away? Please tell them how God helped you to break him."

"Judge," I replied, "I will be happy to serve God and you in this matter. I will do anything I can to help."

I had not met any of these parents before, so what the devil meant for a trap became an open door.

When we got home W. G. was very depressed. He said, "Mama, I want to go far away where no one knows me. Couldn't we please move? I don't want to be called a jailbird!"

"Son," I replied earnestly, "I am the pastor here. God and my superintendent, Brother Stallones, placed me here. I cannot leave until the Lord releases me from this post of duty. But I don't think you need to worry about being called a jailbird. The judge made it very plain that you did not commit a crime. It was merely an accident that you were picked up with that gang. Don't you remember I told you if you weren't guilty and if we prayed God would help you when you faced the judge? Don't you see? God did it! The judge is using your testimony to help those boys from a life of crime. Cheer up, son. I feel happy about it all!"

This boy, about to become a man, was making tremendous strides in maturity. We had only lived in tents before the fire, and W. G. had been infected with the seven-year-itch from the son of an evangelist who was passing through. He had asked me if he could stay home from school and fast and pray. When I asked him why, he told me he did not want to be embarrassed in school by having to scratch all the time. That evening, when he got ready to break his fast, he first sat down in a chair and asked me to anoint him and pray for his healing. When I had done this Elton and each of the others also asked to be anointed and take advantage of W. G.'s fasting for healing. God healed every one of them!

I have never had any experiences in that category again. However, I am aware that each of us has an appointment to stand before the Judge of all nations. If people could only anticipate that inevitable occurrence and prepare themselves, they would certainly have nothing to fear from that righteous Judge. "Shall not the Judge of all the earth do right?" (Genesis 18:25).

Many of my actions have been misinterpreted and people have passed judgment upon me, often unfairly. But rest assured, the Judgment will bring it all to light. "To his own master he standeth or falleth" (Romans 14:4).

Are you ready to face the Judge?

Chapter Thirteen

*M*y *F*irstborn *S*on

"**M**others rest easy. Your sons are safe. I am not going to take this country into war!"

The radios and newspapers broadcast these words from the president of the United States. But I did not rest easy. I had two sons and they were ever on my mind. Then I had a dream that contradicted what the president had said. I went to Brother Shindoll, whom I had been assisting for a short while, and told him I believed God had given me the dream to direct me to return to California.

"I want to be with Elton, my firstborn son, before he leaves for war. I believe God has shown me we will be at war shortly, and Elton is the only one of my children who is not filled with the Holy Ghost."

We made the trip to Sacramento, California, as quickly as possible, and immediately upon arrival I was invited to preach a revival in North Sacramento. I really felt that God had opened that door.

While I was preaching that revival Pearl Harbor was

attacked and the United States went to war.

My oldest son, Forrest Elton Ellis, went to war. We always called him Elton because his father's name was Forrest.

While Elton was in training, he had an experience somewhat similar to that of his Grandmother Harris. The army trained Elton in Oregon. One day, after an all-day hike over rugged terrain, the men were permitted to stop around dark to spend the night. They were so bone weary and tired that Elton and his buddy threw one army blanket on the ground and covered up with the second army blanket. They were lying back to back. Elton said his buddy went to sleep almost immediately, but he was just beginning to doze when he felt the unmistakable sensation of a snake coiling between him and the other soldier.

His first instinct was to leap from the pallet and escape the danger, but his next thought was for his friend. He recalled being informed they were in rattlesnake territory, and there was not a doubt in his mind about the size, species, and deadliness of the snake. He could not alert his companion for fear it would strike. His only hope was that the serpent would get too warm and decide to move on. Elton used the same tactic his Grandmother Harris had used years before: he desperately prayed and trusted God.

After what seemed like ages, Elton related, the huge snake, nearly as long as their pallet, slowly began to uncoil and depart. As soon as he felt he could safely do so, Elton alerted his buddy, grabbed a flashlight, and quickly killed the large diamondback rattler.

After training in Oregon, Elton was assigned to

Ft. Benning, Georgia, to train as a paratrooper. I did not know he was being transferred until the Lord revealed it to me in a vision as I prayed in my home in Vallejo. This incident is recorded in my book *Oma and Angels*. Elton walked in while I was still caught up in the vision, and I thought his voice was part of the vision. He was thrilled to know that the Lord had shown me he could safely jump with a parachute, for he had a lifelong fear of heights.

On his last visit home before sailing to war, Elton asked me for the address of a church near Ft. Mead, Maryland. He said he had been issued very heavy clothing so he felt they would be going into a cold climate. Since it was already May, he suspected it might be Greenland or Iceland, though nobody knew for sure.

I received a card from Elton after he returned to his ship. It said, "I will be a long way out to sea by the time you receive this. I had no time to look for a church, as they did not allow us to leave the ship again."

I knew Elton had been concerned about his soul. I was so in hopes that he would find a church in Maryland and receive the Holy Ghost, but his card shattered my hopes. A heavy burden for him settled on my heart.

I had a guest in my home, Sister Mary Durham, one of our ministers. She became disturbed because I spent most of my time on my knees. One night I prayed all night. Sister Mary would awake at intervals and insist that I go to bed and get some rest. The last time she called to me, I replied, "Sister, I can't sleep. I am too burdened for Elton's soul. If I only knew how to reach him, I could tell him we have churches in England if he wants to locate one when he arrives."

Sister Mary asked, "Sister Oma, how do you know he is going to England? I thought he said he didn't know but he thought it would be a cold country."

I had no answer for her, but I stayed on my knees.

Around 4:00 A.M. my telephone rang. I rushed to the phone wondering who would be calling at that hour of the morning. A voice said, "Telegram for Oma Ellis, please."

"I am Oma Ellis," I assured him.

"Would you like for me to read the message?" the voice asked.

"Please do," I replied.

"It reads, 'Mother, is there something you want to tell me? Send it to this code number. . . . Elton Ellis.' Do you want to answer?" the operator asked.

"Yes," I said. "Elton, we have churches in England. When you arrive there, look for one. Mother."

There was silence for a moment as if the operator had covered the mouthpiece. I heard a very faint voice say, "How in the world could she know where that ship is going? We don't even know that. We are at war. Such things as that are kept secret!"

"Mrs. Ellis," asked the operator, "is that all of your message?"

"Yes, but will you know if my son's ship receives the message?"

"We will know," he replied. "If they do not, I will notify you."

When I hung up the phone I knew God had heard my prayers. I soon fell into bed and had many hours of restful sleep. I don't know how much that built my character, but it sure did build my faith!

From that time on God kept me informed, as I prayed, about my son's whereabouts, condition, and activities. It was amazing to some and unbelievable to others. But my God supplied information I needed even if it was top secret!

When Elton returned from the war he filled in other details. He left Camp Kilmer, New Jersey, on June 16, 1944. He arrived in Liverpool, England (just as the Lord had revealed to me) on June 27, 1944. The troops landed assault boats on Omaha Beach, Normandy, and pressed their way until they reached Belgium around the first of September. On September 4, 1944, Elton's unit made a nighttime river crossing and reached two miles behind the German enemy lines. On his 23rd birthday, September 6, he was wounded and taken prisoner. His captors placed him in the Luftwaffe (Nazi air force) hospital in Germany.

At that time the army sent me a telegram delivered by a man and a woman, informing me that Elton was missing in action. This episode is also described in *Oma and Angels*. They were upset because I told them the Lord had shown me that Elton was alive.

Later, the Lord showed me that Elton was in a prison and told me that location. It seemed our government had no listing of its location, but my God knew! He was near Stettin, in western Poland.

When the Russians entered Stettin on March 8, 1945, the Germans marched Elton and the other prisoners west and south until April 13, 1945, then abandoned them. Elton told me, just while I was writing this manuscript, that soon after abandonment they met up with an American engineer battalion. They were then flown by C–47's back to the coast of France at Le Havre. They were fed there after being starved for so long. (Even today, more than forty years later, Elton's stomach is so drawn up he cannot eat a normal-size meal.) They got shaves, baths, and new uniforms. They had lived for eight months in the battlefield uniforms in which they were wounded—bloody, dirty, and lice infested.

Elton's injuries disqualified him for further war service, so a Liberty ship brought him back to the States, arriving May 13, 1945.

I was teaching in a Bible college at Caldwell, Idaho. I was greatly encouraged during those war years to hear our students praying. At any time when they asked leave to go aside and pray we always excused them from classes. God proved He was well pleased with this practice, for He sent angels to visit our school. When Brother Emmanuel Rohn, the school's president, saw the angels above the heads of the student body as he was speaking, he became unable to speak. Some students said he looked like white marble stone; others said he seemed transfigured, with a white glistening light changing his features. When Brother Rohn told them what he had beheld there was great rejoicing.

But on May 13, 1945, it was my turn to rejoice. When I was called to the phone and heard Elton's voice, all heaven burst in my heart. The students thought I had gone crazy. My joy was not only over Elton's return but also over the fact that my God had proved Himself faithful to me.

My firstborn son. We have been through so much together. At this writing Elton is still my only child who has not received the Holy Ghost. That is certainly no blot against his character, for all his life people have noticed his remarkable manners and steadfast loyalty. Once, when he was only eighteen or nineteen years old I let him use the car to take people to a special service that night. Somebody asked me why I let him use the car. I told them I let him use it because I could trust him to return it. Sure enough, he drove up while we were talking.

I knew a man several years ago, the most similar man to Elton I have ever met. He was of sterling character. Everyone spoke highly of him. Businessmen complimented him to me, his pastor. They said he was a person of proper conduct, honorable, noble, upright, and honest.

In fact, his boss, the general manager of the store, told me one day, "Mrs. Ellis, your church seems to be producing wonderful Christians. My assistant manager is the most perfect man of God I have ever known. Are all the men in the church like him?"

I could only say, "He has the most beautiful character, in appearance, of any man I have ever met. And yes, we do have some wonderful Holy Ghost–filled men in our congregation."

How could I explain to this businessman that moral character does not assure that a man is saved? This classification is a danger to the individual himself.

From that time on, in 1947, I placed that man at the top of my prayer list. I urged him to seek God until he received the Spirit so he could live up to what his boss thought him to be.

I refreshed his memory of the biblical requirements of repentance, baptism in Jesus' name, and the infilling of the Holy Ghost, speaking in tongues. I quoted John 3:3, 5, 7; Acts 2:38; and Acts 4:12 until I know he must have memorized them. After that he seemed to make a greater effort. He had a godly mother who reared him to be such a commendable person, but she carried a great burden for his soul because she knew he could not be saved without being born again.

I began to suspect the man's own self-righteousness was his hindrance. What his problem was I do not know, but finally, after thirty-two years, he received the Holy Ghost in 1979!

The Bible teaches about two births and two deaths. If we are born naturally and then born again, we only have to die the natural death, because the second death has no power on us (Revelation 20:6). However, if we are born naturally and never receive the new birth, then we must die twice—the natural death and the second death, which the Bible describes as the lake of fire (Revelation 20:14). Somebody coined the phrase "Born once, die twice; born twice, die once."

Once, when I was urging Elton to seek God more earnestly for the Holy Ghost, he pointed out two young men in the church about his age who had made mistakes. I explained that many young Christians make mistakes in the process of learning. But Elton felt he had to get to the place where he knew he could live a Holy Ghost life before he got into the church. For, said he, "I don't ever want to be a hypocrite!"

But both of those young men whom he pointed out were teachable, and they went on to pastor churches and labor for God.

My Grandfather Harris prayed a prayer over me before I was ever born. I didn't even know he prayed the prayer until twenty-three years later. But God honored that prayer. If God answers prayers even after the prayer warrior has passed off the scene of action, I am sure He will honor the hours I have travailed for my children, especially Elton, because of his unregenerate condition. Too many tears have flooded my cheeks, too many miracles already granted. I am therefore asking for one last miracle: salvation for my firstborn son!

Oma and son Elton after he came home from prison camp.

HEADQUARTERS ARMY SERVICE FORCES
OFFICE OF THE PROVOST MARSHAL GENERAL
WASHINGTON 25, D. C.

9 February 1945

> Re: Pvt. Forrest E. Ellis,
> United States Prisoner of War #150061,
> Stalag 2 A, Germany,
> Via: New York, New York.

Mrs. Oma Ellis,
1202 Solano Ave,
Vallejo, California.

Dear Mrs. Ellis:

The Provost Marshal General has directed me to inform you that the above-named prisoner of war has been reported interned at the place indicated.

You may communicate with him by following instructions in the inclosed circular.

One parcel label and two tobacco labels will be forwarded to you every sixty days without application on your part. Labels for the current period will be forwarded under separate cover with the least practicable delay.

Further information will be forwarded as soon as it is received.

Sincerely yours,

Howard F. Bresee

Howard F. Bresee,
Colonel, C.M.P., Director,
American prisoner of War Information Bureau.

Incls.
     Mailing Circular,
     Information Circular.

$\mathscr{L}$OOKING $\mathscr{B}$ACK

N early every home has a special place to put odds and ends. It may be a special drawer in the kitchen or bedroom or a box in the bottom of the closet. That is where things wind up that have no major category.

This chapter is my miscellaneous department. Bringing this book to a close has been difficult because I wanted to remember all the stories my friends and family have enjoyed over the years. Here are the gleanings from the life of a ninety-year-old woman who, in looking back, sees more than could ever be included in one small volume.

Never Break a Vow

Sixty years ago in Dallas, Texas, I knew a remarkable couple who belonged to Brother Matlock's church where I assisted the pastor and taught Sunday school. The Bosmans were quite a contrast. John was a large, husky man. His wife was very tiny, small in stature but not in the Lord. I've used Sister Bosman's testimony many times over the years.

It started with a prayer meeting when she was a young woman. She wanted power with God, power to serve Him as did Elijah and Elisha. As she prayed, she said, "Lord, I want to keep my eyes upon you just like Elisha kept his eyes upon Elijah!" She went on to ask God for power to resist the trials and temptations of life. In her fervency, she testified, she cast about in her mind for something to show how sincerely she wanted these petitions to be answered. She said, "If you will grant these requests, Lord, I promise to fast every Sunday for the rest of my life!"

I have always taught that one should never lightly make a vow. It is a dangerous thing to do if it isn't kept. "Better is it that thou shouldest not vow, than that thou shouldest vow and not pay" (Ecclesiastes 5:5). Vows make an impact on our lives. For some people, the making and keeping of a vow in the fear of God helps them to maintain their faith and therefore their salvation. For others, the breaking of a vow overwhelms them because they regarded the vow too lightly.

Also in the category of vows are promises. We should be very careful to keep our promises to our fellow man. Unkept promises are lies, and liars have no place in heaven (Revelation 21:27). We will answer to God for everything. As our characters are shaped, we in turn affect the lives of others. "None of us liveth to himself, and no man dieth to himself" (Romans 14:7).

Many years after Sister Bosman pleaded with God for power, she learned how truly God had answered her prayer. She had faithfully kept her vow of fasting on Sundays. One day, she and her husband went out to pick wild blackberries. Sister Bosman crawled into a very close place where the blackberries were plentiful and lush but also very, very thorny. She was not in view of her husband. Suddenly, she spotted a very large diamondback rattler already coiled in some dead leaves close to her head. There was no time to call for John. She realized the thing was going to strike her in the face. Instantly she reached out, rebuking the rattler in Jesus' name, and closed her small hands around the snake's head. At that moment she experienced great strength and power, enabling her to hold on to such a serpent.

Sister Bosman cried out for her husband to come and pull her from the blackberry bushes. Her clothing was caught securely in the briers.

Unaware of the deadly struggle, John goodnaturedly complained about the situations women can get themselves into. He found the job not too easy. Trying to extract her from those bushes was a chore until he suddenly realized his wife was clinging to an enormous, writhing reptile. The rescue took on a different aspect after that! He immediately jerked her free from the briers and killed her deadly foe.

Later, John was incredulous. Over and over he would shake his head and say, "How did she do it? It had to be God."

Sister Bosman would smile and say, "I will always believe it was the keeping of my vow that saved my life. I have never had that kind of strength in my body as God gave me to wrestle that snake."

I also believe God honored Sister Bosman's vow. He will honor anybody who makes a vow out of deep consecration and keeps it.

A Vow of Holiness

The Lord allowed me to overhear a woman make a vow back in 1931. It was a joy to witness, for I had prayed many times about the situation.

The young lady was a member of the church I pioneered in Somerton, Arizona. The dress styles of that era were not what a consecrated Christian should wear. But they appealed to this sister, and she yielded to the temptation. She had even gone so far in her backsliding as to cut her hair.

The situation was very stressful for me, because I feared I was not presenting the holiness message in a manner to reach her. I fasted and prayed, asking the Lord to give me wisdom.

There was a lot of unrest in the nation. We were in the grips of a depression, with wages so low that poor people could hardly live. Strikes were numerous and dangerous. As I used these things in a Bible study to point out that we were in perilous times, many people were stirred, but not this sister.

One man inserted a comment on my lesson, "Sister Ellis, the Bible says that in the last days there will be perilous times and men will not endure sound doctrine." (See II Timothy 3:1; 4:3.) "All these are things to warn us to take heed to our ways, for everyone shall be judged by God's holy Word; we should allow these Scriptures we've heard here tonight to direct us in the way we dress, in our actions, and in our doings. God is holy and He expects His people to be holy." Even this sincere proclamation failed to visibly stir our erring friend.

A few days later I was visiting in the home of her parents when several truckloads of strikers with shotguns surrounded her father's fields. In the fields were a large number of people harvesting his vegetable crop. The strikers ordered the laborers to leave the field or suffer the consequences. They began to fire the shotguns over the workers' heads as warnings.

Those of us in the house rushed out to a nearby knoll when we heard the gunshots. The father was not present, and the women were frantic and screaming, because several people had been killed in earlier strikes. The daughter who had been losing her consecration ran by me as I stood watching and praying. I heard her in an agonized voice say, "O Lord! Not now. Please wait until my hair grows out! Please! Please! Dear God, don't come now!"

In her sudden fear her failures rose to torment her. She quickly renewed her consecration and dedicated herself to God. As long as I knew her she kept her vow. I hope she keeps it until the end. No one will have time to repent when Jesus comes, for His coming will be in the twinkling of an eye. (See I Corinthians 15:52.) "Therefore be ye also ready: for in such an hour as ye think not the Son of man cometh" (Matthew 24:44).

Fourteen Years in the Desert

I have many fond memories of the time I spent in Arizona. It was hot, dry, desert land, but the blessings of the Lord flowed like a river.

I remember with gratitude the help given me by the Long family. I called Brother Cecil Long "my right-hand man." Melba Long, Cecil's wife, was the president of our Ladies Auxiliary and became expert in making the pie dough for our half-moon fried pies. We had many fund raisers, but none as successful as those delicious pies. Sister Smart, an evangelist in our church, had a job at the courthouse. She would take those hot pies to work with her, and they proved to be terrific sellers. My granddaughter, Sharon Cox (now Sharon Ikerd, a missionary to Africa), went from door to door with a basket of fried pies on her arm. Though only a child, she was our top saleslady!

The ladies met me every Saturday at 10:00 A.M. for prayer meeting. I have always taught, "Little prayer, little power; much prayer, much power." And God did bless us with mighty miracles.

The Langeneggers labored long hours helping me install coolers. We spent some miserable hours squatting on the two-by-fours in the attic, but they stuck it out with me.

Several years before we got the church finished, George Sponsler's mother from Visalia, California, gave me several shrubs, trees, and vines from her nursery to beautify the church and parsonage grounds. I dearly loved them. I rose early every day to water them, and sometimes late at night. Very few others even attempted to grow anything.

After we finished our building program the Phoenix church choir came for a program of music and singing. They asked me to rent an organ to be used with our piano. I made arrangements with the owner of a downtown Yuma music store, and he came with those who made the delivery. He was a member of the largest and finest church in the city.

When he stepped inside, he stopped short and looked over everything. He said, "Mrs. Ellis, I have passed by this place many times. It looks like a beautiful, green oasis in the midst of this dry desert. For a long time I've wanted to see the inside of this building. This is the neatest church in our city. That shows that someone cares, lady!''

Now, in my old age, that compliment comes back to warm my heart and fill me with appreciation for God's blessings.

Surprise Visitors

When I was nearing sixty years of age I had picked up a few pounds more than I weighed when the Langeneggers and I worked in the church attic. I had recently remodeled the parsonage, and a rain had revealed a few leaks in the ceiling. I decided I'd better get those leaks repaired before the next rain ruined my pretty, newly painted ceilings. (Yes, it does rain sometimes in that dry desert!)

I had to go through a crawl hole in the top of a linen closet that faced the living room and front door. Taking some straws or toothpicks to stick in the cracks I felt the sunshine would reveal, I found the job every bit as exhausting and tedious as the work had been in the church attic.

A loud knock at the front door interrupted the ordeal of my old limbs and hurting knees. I stuck my head down through the hole and yelled, "Come in," thinking it was some of the sisters from the church.

Who should walk in but Brother Clyde Haney, founder of the Bible college at Stockton, California, and with him was the superintendent of the Arizona District! When they looked up and saw my head hanging down from the ceiling they both had a hearty laugh over my predicament.

"What in the world are you doing, Sister Ellis?" they asked.

I had known these brethren for years. I replied, "I'm up in this attic locating leaks so I can go on top of the roof and do some repairs. There was no one else here to do it today."

"So you have become the maintenance worker for the U.P.C. of Yuma!" they teased. "We came to talk to you. Do you suppose you can come down long enough for us to tell you what we have on our minds?"

I said, "Brethren, I cannot make my descent graceful by any means. I will not come down while you are gawking at me. Please go to the kitchen," I laughed, "while I get down!"

They marched to the kitchen, still teasing, saying, "This is one time we will allow the woman to rule over the man."

Low Spot

They say, "When it rains, it pours." My exodus from Tugglesville, California, was one of the low spots of my life.

My brother Jesse and Elton left for work, most of the young ministers left, and many of the people left during the cotton-gathering season. One man who didn't leave was a minister in good standing, except he didn't believe in women pastors. He was causing a lot of unrest, circulating amongst the people. In the midst of it, Brother Stallones died, and it was the proverbial straw that broke the camel's back. I simply caved in, unable and unwilling to try to hold the group together without Brother Stallones's assistance.

In my mind I had a perfect right to be pastor under the officials whom God had ordained to govern the church (I Corinthians 12:23-28). Spiritually, "there is neither male nor female: for ye are all one in Christ Jesus" (Galatians 3:28). As long as I was subject to Brother Stallones and the Lord, I felt qualified to lead that precious band of saints, but I could not bear to see them split up. So I decided to resign and let them give the church to the brother who was so against me. I went with an absolutely broken heart.

Years later, that brother met me at a conference and asked me to forgive him. I assured him he was forgiven before I ever left. A short time later he died. I was so happy we had that conversation.

Looking back, I hope there's nothing between my soul and the Savior!

$\mathcal{T}$HE $\mathcal{B}$EST $\mathcal{T}$ILL $\mathcal{L}$AST

From the low point of the former chapter, where I left Tugglesville, California, with a very heavy heart, the Lord soon blessed me with a high point. My oldest child, LaJuan, was the one in the spotlight in this adventure.

On Fire for Jesus

The trip to Oklahoma had been plagued with car trouble. But that was nothing to the trouble that awaited us just over the hill. Pearl Cox was at the wheel; her mother and I were in the front seat with her. In the back seat were my three children and another teenager named Lily Mae. It was late in the evening on the third day of our journey when we started down a very steep incline into the desert plains of New Mexico.

Suddenly, the left front tire blew out, throwing the car into a figure eight. On both sides of the highway were deep embankments, but Pearl managed to keep the car on the road. Not a word had been spoken, except both Sister Cox and I had said, "Jesus, Jesus!"—very calmly to keep down panic. When the car came to rest it was pointed west where we'd come from. From under the front seat fire erupted, so we all piled quickly out of the car. Spilled gas from the gas tank also ignited.

Directly behind us had been a Greyhound bus. The driver was on the scene immediately with a fire extinguisher and had the fire extinguished in a very short time. As the bus was leaving the driver told me he would send a wrecker from about forty miles away to drag our car in for repairs. He warned me that he had heard they charged unreasonable prices. I had no other choice but to approve his suggestion.

Another car had been driving ahead of us, and its occupants saw the accident in their rear-view mirror. By the time they returned, LaJuan had everything that had been packed in the trunk thrown down the nearest embankment. She told us later she had grabbed the keys from Pearl when we all piled out and directed the teenagers in emptying the contents of the trunk. The memory of losing everything when our tent had burned was fresh in her mind, and she was determined to save our clothing and such things as we now possessed.

As our fellow travelers arrived at the scene of the accident one man asked, "Where is the other car?"

LaJuan answered, "We only have one car."

"I can't believe all of that stuff came out of one car trunk," the gentleman exclaimed.

"Well, it did," replied LaJuan, "and I'm going to put it all back again."

While the men watched in amazement as she repacked

the car, LaJuan testified to them. She told them her mom was a Pentecostal preacher and she traveled with her and had much practice in packing.

They watched the job well done. But the last few things they could not believe LaJuan would find a spot to put them. Each item was successfully stored and the trunk closed, much to their surprise. The man walked away shaking his head and saying, "Nobody but you could ever have done that!"

Now we had time to praise the Lord as we waited for the wrecker. The bus driver had told us he fully expected us to go over the embankment and burn to death. He thought we were very fortunate. We believed we were blessed. But that is not the high point to which I made reference.

The wrecker driver found us all in a joyful mood even though we needed another tire, two battery cables, and towing fee. He asked me to ride in the wrecker so we could discuss the repairs. In a little while he asked who we were and where we were going. This opened the door for me to witness to him of God's saving grace. All who know me will believe me when I say I took full advantage of the time to preach Jesus to him. In the meantime, in the car that was being towed, that old prayer warrior Sister Cox was in intercessory prayer for God to supply our needs.

Those forty miles were the highlight of many, many days. It was the most enjoyable thing that had happened since I'd left my heart at Tugglesville.

After the car was repaired and I got ready, by faith, to pay the bill, he said, "The towing bill is free. I so enjoyed our conversation. It isn't often I get to hear anything like that. The tire didn't cost me anything, so I'll give that to you. The patch on the inner tube cost twenty-five cents, and I charge fifty cents to put on a patch, so you owe me seventy-five cents.''

When we arrived in Vinson, Oklahoma, I stepped right into a pulpit. God knows that the best thing for a grieving mother is more children. As long as I was in Vinson I had newborn saints again to pastor.

I always wanted to be on fire for Jesus. But that one fiery experience on the highway was enough for me!

Dedicated with Love

Our church in Rapid City was without a pastor for two months when I was past eighty-eight years old and bedfast. We hated to see our pastor go, but he felt he was in the will of God. He came to see me often and was so kind to me. His wife also was precious and such a comfort. The Lord gave us a new pastor who also was a blessing, urging me to help him counsel and pray for folks.

In the interim, before we got our new pastor, I was asked to dedicate a baby. I hesitated, telling the family to wait for the new pastor. They argued that the grandparents were there and wanted to witness the dedication. It was then I remembered that my Grandfather Harris dedicated me from his sickbed. The little ceremony was very precious to me.

Later, I dedicated another little fellow. The next week while visiting in the home of the Ueckers, my caretakers, the little boy got in trouble and his father carried him into my room. I asked if he had a smile to replace that frown. His daddy said he might have one in his pocket. With tears still streaming down his sweet little face, his chubby fingers groped until they found that smile and put it on his face. He was surprised when we all burst out laughing.

It's moments like this that make me thank God for a long life full of laughter, and yes, tears. But it's been a good life living for the Lord!

Then, there are moments when I contemplate the death of my daughter Jackie. The Lord let me have a good visit with her before her passing. Jackie received the Holy Ghost in 1938 in that Tugglesville revival.

Calls and letters come in and brighten my days. Like the call from the wife of the Canadian cabinet member. She had read two of my books and called with a prayer request.

The weekly calls from Elton—I look forward to them so much.

But I saved the best till last.

A Letter from My Brother Bill

On October 30, 1987, I received a letter from my oldest brother, Bill Francis, and his wife, Dee. It is one of my cherished possessions.

It reads:

Dear Oma,

I love you for leading Dee and me to the Lord. Don't know if we would have found the truth and been filled with the Holy Ghost if it hadn't been for you. . . .

His letter caused my mind to go back to 1923, when I received the Holy Ghost and immediately began to write to them about how wonderful it was to be filled with God's Spirit. They told me after they were converted that my letters were disgusting to them and they seldom read all of them. They all seemed like sermons and they just weren't interested.

A few days before a severe family squabble, another of my letters had arrived. They had only partially read it and pitched it behind an old trunk. In the midst of their terrible argument, which was leading toward a separation, Bill remembered something I had said in the letter. He dug it out and read it all the way through, commenting to Dee, "If that Holy Ghost can do what Oma says it can, it's what we both need. Let's go see Oma and talk to her about it!"

And so they came. And that Holy Ghost did what Oma said it could!

This is the story of my life in a nutshell: to lead someone to a saving knowledge of Jesus Christ.

Bill's letter made me cry. Not tears of sorrow, but tears of joy. If there were not another page that could be written about my life, this page would be worth it all. To lead my brother to the Lord is quite a reward.

Oma age 91 with Sunday school in Mitchell, South Dakota before having a picnic.

Four generations: Back row: Lee Etta Ikerd, LaJuan Sanders, Michael O'Neal, Kelli O'Neal. Front row: Donald Ikerd, Sharon Ikerd, Beth Ikerd, Keith Ikerd. The two boys in laps are Oma's great-great grandsons, Michael Shane O'Neal and Jordan Ikerd.

Oma Ellis' 90th Birthday at Rapid City, South Dakota. This was the last visit with her daughter Jackie and Jackie's children from California. Jackie died in March, 1990 and her son Terry Wyatt died in January 1991. Back row: Terry Wyatt, Jackie Wyatt, LaJuan Sanders, John Sanders, Denise Uecker, Dennis B. Uecker, Fern Uecker. Front row: Kim Heydt, Pam Heydt, Leslie Wyatt, Clayton Wyatt, Oma Ellis, Dennis M. Uecker.